GARDENING
HACKS

D1390842

GARDENING HACKS

An Hachette UK Company
www.hachette.co.uk

Summersdale Publishers Ltd
Part of Octopus Publishing Group Limited
Carmelite House
50 Victoria Embankment
LONDON
EC4Y 0DZ
UK

www.summersdale.com

Printed and bound in Croatia

ISBN: 978-1-78685-258-8

Substantial discounts on bulk quantities of Summersdale books are available to corporations, professional associations and other organisations. For details contact general enquiries: telephone: +44 (0) 1243 771107 or email: enquiries@summersdale.com.

GARDENING HACKS

Handy Hints to Make Gardening Easier

Seedling for your Monday detox salad

Eggshell from your Friday fry-up

Dan Marshall

Over **130** amazing hacks inside!

summersdale

DISCLAIMER

Neither the author nor the publisher can be held responsible for any loss or claim arising out of the use, or misuse, of the suggestions made herein.

CONTENTS

Introduction.....................................7

Planting Hacks...............................8

Flower-Tending Hacks.....................23

Plant-Health Hacks........................36

Pest-Control Hacks.........................47

Veggie-Patch Hacks........................61

Tree and Bush Hacks......................75

Garden-Decoration Hacks..............88

Wild Flower Hacks........................101

Weeding Hacks.............................114

Tool Hacks....................................127

Planning and Organising Hacks.....139

Shed and Greenhouse Hacks.........152

Wildlife-Garden Hacks..................163

Lawn Hacks..................................176

If All Else Fails.............................186

Final Word...................................187

Hacks Index.................................188

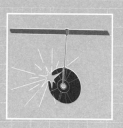

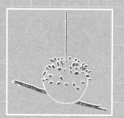

INTRODUCTION

Ah, the garden. It's the place where you want to relax at the end of a hard day, but if that hard day has been spent toiling over the lawn, grappling with weeds and searching the shed for your missing rake, you may begin to feel that your garden is more trouble than it's worth. Well, fear not – your days of spending hours on garden maintenance are over. This book contains over 130 cunning gardening tips that will save you time, trouble and money, *and* help you to achieve the garden of your dreams.

From planting a productive veggie patch to outwitting evil slugs, *Gardening Hacks* has got it covered. If you want to know how a nappy can save you time watering and a ruler can help you get rid of stubborn weeds, read on. By the end of this book you'll have much more time to enjoy your garden, but it'll look as though you've been slaving away over a spade for weeks… we won't tell if you don't! After all, our philosophy here at Life Hacks Towers is 'maximum results for minimum effort'. So pick up your tools and get hacking!

PLANTING HACKS

Are you struggling to get newly planted seeds to germinate, or worrying about your seedlings getting enough water? Planting, propagating and transplanting can be tricky, so check out these stress-free hacks to make sure your leafy offspring get the best start in life.

EGGSHELL PLANTERS

Don't shell out on expensive biodegradable pots for your seedlings – try this quick and easy hack instead.

Just save and rinse your eggshells, pierce a small hole in the bottom of each and fill with compost. Pop in your seed and mist with a plant spray once a day. When your seedlings are ready to plant out, crack the shells gently and transfer straight to the ground. Your egg pot will biodegrade and even add calcium to the surrounding soil. How's that for a cracking idea?

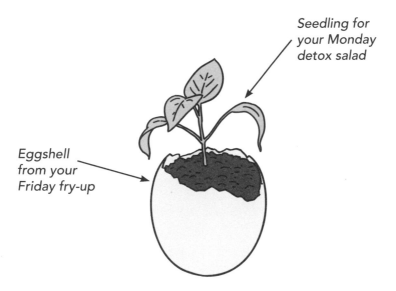

Seedling for your Monday detox salad

Eggshell from your Friday fry-up

DIY SOIL-TYPE TEST

How can you tell if your soil is acidic or alkaline without calling in CSI? This hack shows you – lab coat and goggles are optional.

Find two bowls and put a cup of soil in each. Add enough water to turn the soil to mud. To test for alkaline soil, add ½ a cup of vinegar to one bowl and stir. If the sample fizzes your soil is alkaline. To test for acidic soil, add ½ a cup of baking soda to the other bowl. Stir, and if there is a reaction your soil is acidic. If neither reacts, you have neutral soil – lucky you!

Baking soda, reacts with acidic soil

Vinegar, reacts with alkaline soil

Mud, glorious mud

Mud

SANDY SEED SOLUTION

One of the miracles of gardening is the way mahoosive plants grow from the smallest seeds, but some of those seeds are *really* tiny, aren't they? If you're struggling to plant your mini-miracle seeds evenly, this tip is for you.

Place your seeds in a dry container and add some sand – nine parts sand to one part seed (measured by weight) works well. Mix the seeds in, then sprinkle the mix along your row. You'll get a good even distribution without your seeds clumping together in one place, and it'll be easier to see where you're planting, too!

Sand + seeds = handy sandy mix

WINE-CORK SEED DIBBER

If you're planting up lots of seed trays, it makes sense to use a dibber that can make several holes at once. And if you're fond of a glass of wine – and who isn't? – it also makes sense to make your own dibber using recycled corks. Here's how.

Find a ruler (a metal one will work best for this method, but it could be substituted if you don't have one) and grab four wine corks. Glue the corks along the flat side of the ruler to make four perfectly spaced holes for your seed-tray size. Once the glue has set you'll be ready to dib 16 holes in under 5 seconds… which leaves a little extra time to relax with a glass of wine.

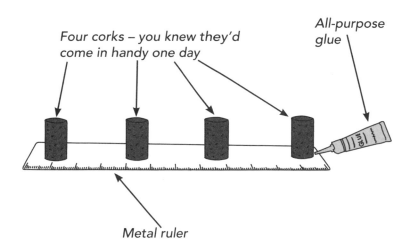

Four corks – you knew they'd come in handy one day

All-purpose glue

Metal ruler

BERRY-BOX GREENHOUSE

These micro-greenhouses must be the easiest hack in this book.

Simply rinse out the containers you buy berries in, remove any light-blocking labels, add some seed compost (to about three-quarters full) and plant your seeds as per the instructions on the pack. Your seedlings will have a warm yet ventilated home until they are strong enough to go it alone. Cheap, easy and super effective – the perfect hack!

Perfect propagator

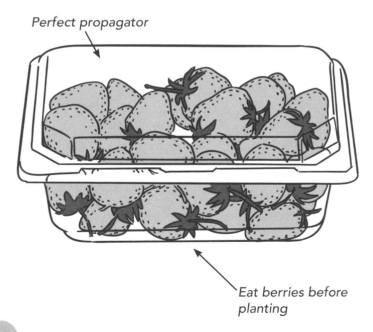

Eat berries before planting

EASY IRRIGATION SYSTEM

Here's a great way to recycle plastic bottles and enrich your plants at the same time.

In dry weather, it can be hard for water to get down to the roots of your bigger plants, so take an empty drinks bottle and pierce holes all over it with a skewer, then bury it next to your plant with the top just poking out above the soil. Fill the bottle with water and it will gradually be released where your plant needs it most – deep down at its roots. Brilliant!

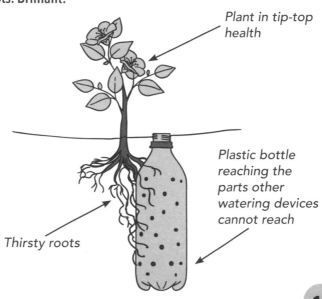

Plant in tip-top health

Plastic bottle reaching the parts other watering devices cannot reach

Thirsty roots

HONEY ROOTING REMEDY

If you were a tiny cutting, recently severed from your parent plant, you'd need a little something to get over the shock, right? Well, try this easy hack to make your own natural rooting solution and settle your traumatised cuttings.

Boil two cups of water and stir in a tablespoon of honey. Let the mixture cool and store in a jar. When ready to root your cuttings, decant some of the solution into a cup and dip the tip of your cutting in it before planting. The honey gives cuttings an energy boost and guards against bacterial problems too. Sweet!

Honey

Comforted
cutting

NAPPY WATER RETAINER

Watering your hanging baskets is a bit of a chore, but this hack will stop them from drying out too quickly.

Take a couple of nappies – yes, you read that right! – and pierce two or three holes in them for drainage. Lay them with the absorbent side up in the base of your hanging basket, fill with soil and plant as usual. The nappies contain the same water-storing crystals that you can buy at the garden centre and will keep your soil moist for just as long.

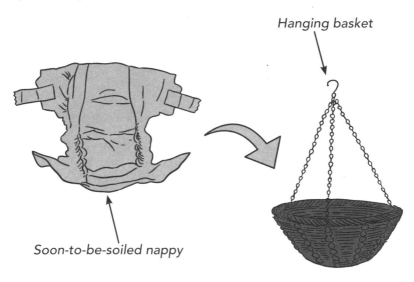

Hanging basket

Soon-to-be-soiled nappy

EPSOM SALTS SHOCK ABSORBER

Moving house is always stressful and it's no different if you're a plant. Avoid transplantation shock by giving your greenery a dose of Epsom salts on moving day.

Mix one tablespoon of Epsom salts into a gallon (4.5 litres) of water and saturate the soil where you're planning to put your plant. (Top tip: water normally first, so that your mixture doesn't disappear into the dry soil, then saturate with your Epsom mix once the soil is damp.) Water again once your plant is in situ and it'll survive relocation with no problems at all.

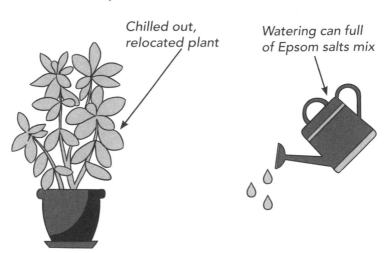

Chilled out, relocated plant

Watering can full of Epsom salts mix

STOCKING PLANT-TIES

Like most of us, plants need a little support now and then. This great hack shows you how to make your own plant ties from that pair of laddered tights languishing at the back of the underwear drawer. (What they're doing there is your own damn business.)

Find a pair of sharp scissors and bid your nylons a fond farewell. Cut them into shorter strips and use these to secure your tomatoes. The soft fabric will support your plants without damaging them. No wonder they call them hold-ups!

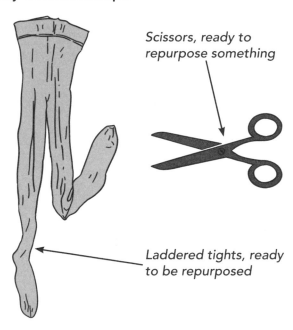

Scissors, ready to repurpose something

Laddered tights, ready to be repurposed

FRIDGE-TOP GERMINATION STATION

You *could* buy yourself a heat pad to help your lovingly planted seeds germinate… or you could try this tip and make the most of naturally occurring warm spots around your home.

Put your seed trays on top of the fridge and they'll germinate more quickly – while your fridge is keeping your salad cool, it's warming up your seedlings at the same time! (Just make sure you're not blocking any vents or causing a fire risk – that would be taking the whole heating-seeds-up thing a bit too far!)

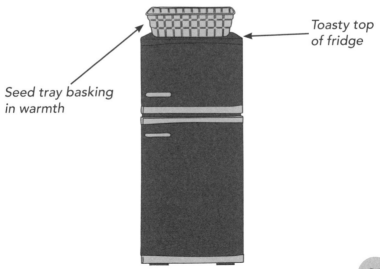

Toasty top of fridge

Seed tray basking in warmth

CUT-AND-DRIED SUCCULENT SUCCESS

There's a secret to propagating succulents – here's how to get an endless supply of the little suckers.

Remove a few leaves from your parent plant (close to the stem), but don't plunge them into a pot straightaway. If you let them dry out for several days first, the cut ends can heal and they won't be able to absorb too much water. Next, lay your leaves on top of some soil and mist it with water whenever it gets dry. Wait for roots to form and *then* gently plant out for super-successful baby succulents.

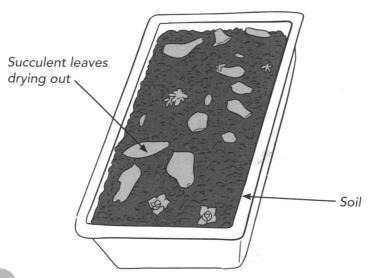

Succulent leaves drying out

Soil

FLOWER-TENDING HACKS

Like children and pets, flowers can be very demanding. They do like the right nutrients, just enough water and a specific soil type, but they don't like frost or being obliterated with a torrent from your watering can – they're such divas! Well, don't despair: here are a host of hacks to keep your flowers blooming marvellously.

MAX YOUR BLOOMS

If you want to enjoy as many flowers as possible from your favourite plants, this hack is for you.

'Deadheading' is not a new concept, but worth mentioning here to inspire you to actually do it! Removing dead or dying flowers will trick your plants into producing new blooms. When flowers fade, just cut them off with a pair of secateurs. (Cut back to the next bud or leaf or, with roses, pinch off the flower head for the best results.) Your perplexed plants will produce more flowers for you to enjoy, rather than going to seed.

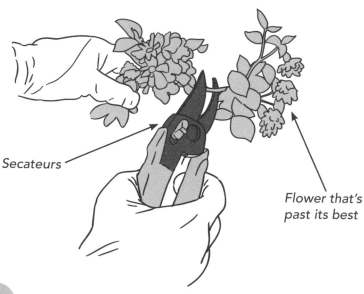

Secateurs

Flower that's past its best

ICE-CUBE ORCHID FIX

Orchids may be beautiful but they're notoriously difficult to care for. One of the biggest dangers is overwatering, so here's a simple hack to ensure that your orchid gets exactly the right amount of water – use an ice cube.

Once a week, place an ice cube on top of the soil next to your orchid and it will water the plant gradually as it melts, without drowning its roots. (For larger orchids, use two ice cubes.) Orchid on the rocks, anyone?

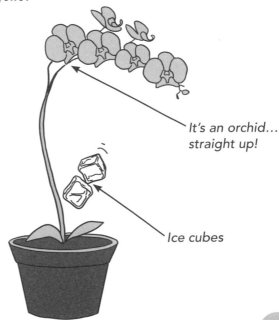

It's an orchid... straight up!

Ice cubes

COMPOST TEA

You need to feed your plants if you want them to produce flashy flowers, but if messing about with manure is not for you try brewing up some 'compost tea' instead.

Fill a large bucket with one-third quality compost and two-thirds water. Leave to stew for three or four days, stirring when possible. Strain the mixture into another bucket (returning the compost to your composter) and your tea is brewed! Use one part tea to ten parts water in your watering can when feeding your plants – serving them cucumber sandwiches is optional.

Good-quality compost

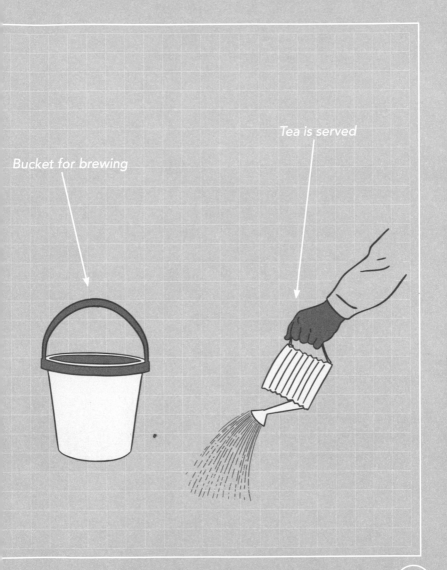

Bucket for brewing

Tea is served

TEA MULCH

It's a well-known fact that most humans are dependent on frequent cups of tea – but did you know that plants can benefit from a daily cuppa too?

Tea contains tannins and other nutrients that will help your flowers to flourish – so mulch your plants with these and you'll get better blooms. Just slit open your used teabags and scatter the tea thinly around your flowers. Blooming marvellous!

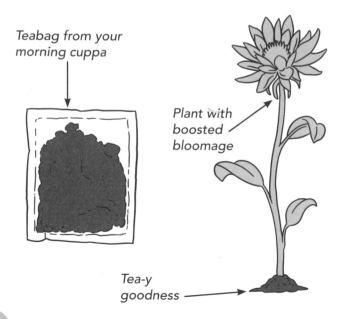

Teabag from your morning cuppa

Plant with boosted bloomage

Tea-y goodness

STICKY-TAPE BUG BLITZER

If your favourite flowers are struck by an aphid attack, a quick blast from the hose can oust them, but chances are it will damage your blooms at the same time. So here's a stealthy way of picking off the enemy using masking tape.

Wrap a short length of tape around your fingers – sticky side out, of course! (I'll pause while you unstick your fingers and start again.) Right, now, gently pat your plant and remove the aphid invaders without damaging so much as a petal in the process.

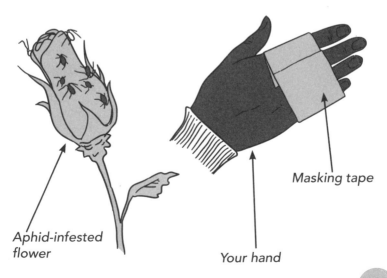

Masking tape

Aphid-infested flower

Your hand

VINEGAR FERTILISER

If you love flowers that need an acidic soil, but don't have that soil type, this hack's for you.

A home-made vinegar fertiliser is a great way to boost your soil's acidity and benefit flowers such as rhododendrons, camellias, hydrangeas and heathers. Simply add a tablespoon of white vinegar to a gallon (4.5 litres) of water and mix well. Water your soil with this once every three months and your acid-happy flowers will flourish.

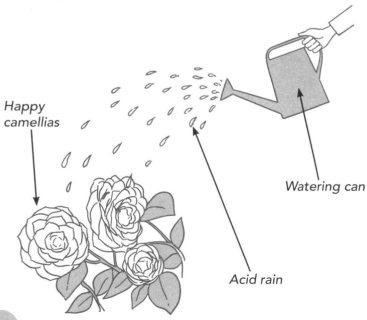

Happy camellias

Watering can

Acid rain

CUT-FLOWER COCKTAIL

Keep cut flowers looking perky for longer with this easy hack. Once you've cut your prize blooms, rest them in a vase of warm water while you mix them a little cocktail to keep them at their best.

Add a few drops of vodka and a teaspoon of sugar to a vase filled with cold water, then arrange your flowers as usual. When they do start to wilt, an extra shot of vodka will perk them up again for a little longer. *Na Zdorovie!*

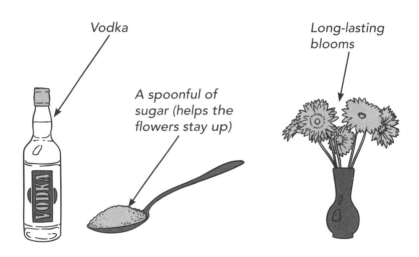

Vodka

A spoonful of sugar (helps the flowers stay up)

Long-lasting blooms

DIY WATERING CAN

Here's a great way to make the perfect watering can for your plants - and you get to choose how fine a spray your can produces.

Use a large, empty milk container and pierce holes in the top with a heated needle. Smaller holes will give you a gentle, fine spray - perfect for watering your more delicate blooms without drowning them or damaging their petals. You can use a drill to make larger holes if you want to water sturdier plants or soak a bigger area.

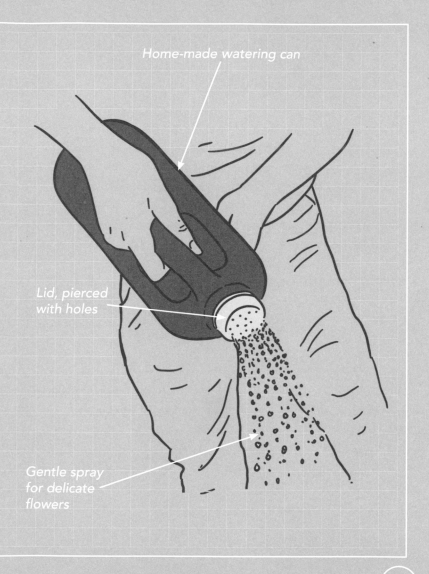

Home-made watering can

Lid, pierced with holes

Gentle spray for delicate flowers

33

SPEEDY BUCKET FROST PROTECTOR

The weather's warmer and you've taken the plunge and planted out your favourite blooms – but what if Mother Nature throws you a curve ball and frost is suddenly on the cards? Fear not – you've got ready-made frost protectors lying around your shed.

Buckets or large plant pots make great frost covers. If frost is looming, pop one over each of your delicate plants and put a brick on top to keep it in place. Don't forget to uncover them in the morning when the weather warms up!

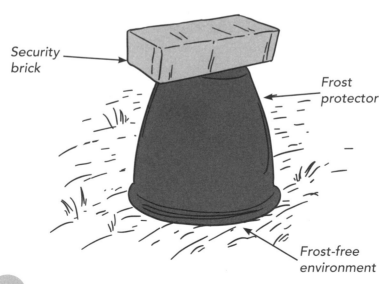

Security brick

Frost protector

Frost-free environment

FIZZY FLOWER TREAT

This is an ingenious way to use up any flat cola you have stashed away in the fridge (fizzy cola works too).

Water plants like azaleas and gardenias with cola once a month and they'll flourish. There's a sciencey reason behind this hack – the sugar in the drink feeds microbes in the soil, leaving more nutrients for your plants, and it will make the soil more acidic too. (Since your plants aren't brand-aware, why not use your supermarket's own cola and save a few pennies.)

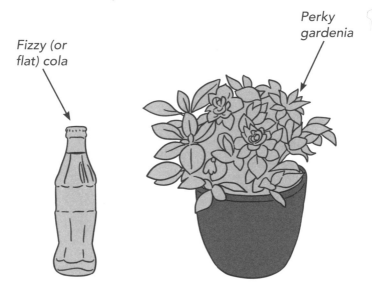

Perky gardenia

Fizzy (or flat) cola

PLANT-HEALTH HACKS

Keeping your plants healthy doesn't have to involve a trip to the garden centre and a bootload of chemicals. This chapter shows you how to become a self-certified plant doctor by using some cunning planting and the contents of your cupboards: beat mildew with milk, perk up your plants with tea-tree oil and spice up your seedlings with cinnamon.

CINNAMON SEEDLING SAVER

Here's a hack to improve your plants' health from day one. Newly planted seeds and seedlings are prone to 'dampening off' – a range of diseases that can turn seeds to mush before they germinate. Stave these nasties off by dusting the soil with powdered cinnamon when planting and you'll see healthy seedlings instead of an empty patch of earth when you check your seed tray in the morning.

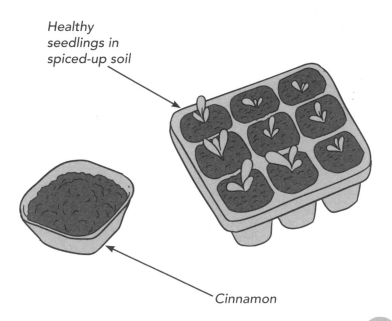

Healthy seedlings in spiced-up soil

Cinnamon

WINTER-COVER SOIL BOOSTER

After a long summer's growing, your soil – like you – is feeling depleted. But if you leave your plot bare throughout the autumn the soil's structure and nutrient levels will suffer. Here's a way to boost nutrient levels with some crafty planting.

Plant your beds with peas or beans in the autumn and they'll protect the soil and add nitrogen to it over winter. Cut down your crops in the spring, a couple of weeks before your main planting (before they flower), and dig this 'green manure' into the soil. You won't get to harvest these crops, but your soil will be replenished and ready for a fruitful season ahead.

Re-energised soil

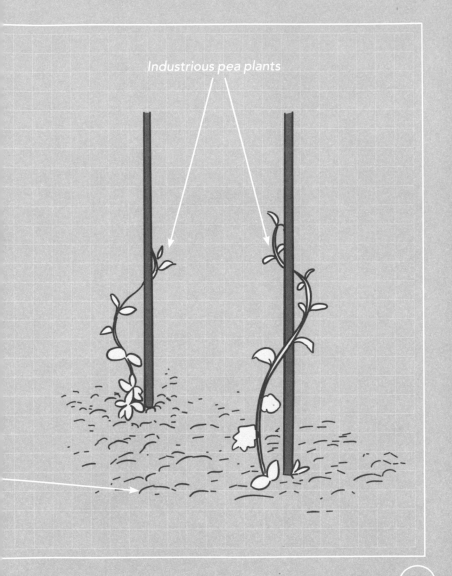

Industrious pea plants

MILKY MILDEW FIX

Courgettes and squashes are susceptible to powdery mildew – but here's a great way to avoid the problem without using chemical sprays and blitzing your bounty.

Just mix three parts milk to seven parts water and pour into a plant spray bottle. Spritz your plants every ten days or so to prevent mildew from forming. (Mix up a fresh batch each time.) The nutrients in milk are great for fertilising your plants too, so you can use the same mix to feed them every couple of weeks and boost your crops.

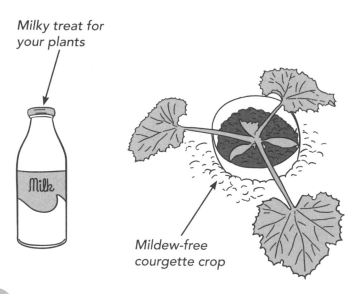

Milky treat for your plants

Mildew-free courgette crop

PASTA-WATER TREAT

Plants love starch, so give them a treat - and do your bit to save the planet - by keeping the water you cook your pasta in and using it to water your plants.

Don't forget to let it cool down first! This tip works well with the cooking water from veggies too - especially potatoes, which are also full of starch. Just make sure that the water isn't salted, which your plants won't appreciate at all.

Tasty tagliatelle

Nutritious cooking water

TEA-TREE TONIC

Around 85 per cent of plant diseases are fungus based – yuck! – so here's a great all-round treatment to have at the ready if you spot any signs of contamination.

Mix a tablespoon of tea-tree oil into a cup of water and pour into a spray bottle. Mist plants twice a week with this to beat their gruesome fungal infections. (Tea-tree oil also deters ants, flies and mosquitoes – the perfect natural pesticide!)

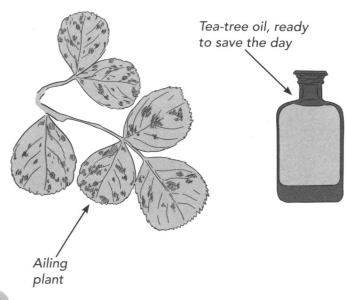

Tea-tree oil, ready to save the day

Ailing plant

PINE-CONE DRAINAGE HACK

Overwatering can lead to wilted plants with yellowing leaves – and no one likes a soggy bottom.

Help prevent this by popping a layer of pine cones into the base of your containers before filling with soil to make sure roots don't become waterlogged. The pine cones will trap pockets of air in the base of your container and will make it lighter too, so it'll be much easier to move around when you're rethinking your patio display!

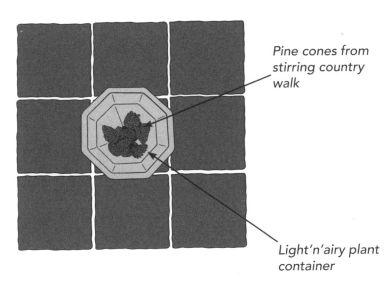

Pine cones from stirring country walk

Light'n'airy plant container

SHADY BOLTING BARRIER

Picture the scene: you haven't picked your greens for a couple of days and you fancy a fresh salad, but when you get to your plot your tasty little lettuces have morphed into 20-foot-tall inedible giants. Plan ahead with some strategic planting to stop your salad veggies turning to compost fodder overnight.

One of the major causes of bolting is too much heat, so plant your mischievous salad crops in the shade of taller plants, such as beans or sweetcorn. They'll be much less likely to run riot and your produce will last for weeks, rather than days.

Tall, shady bean plants

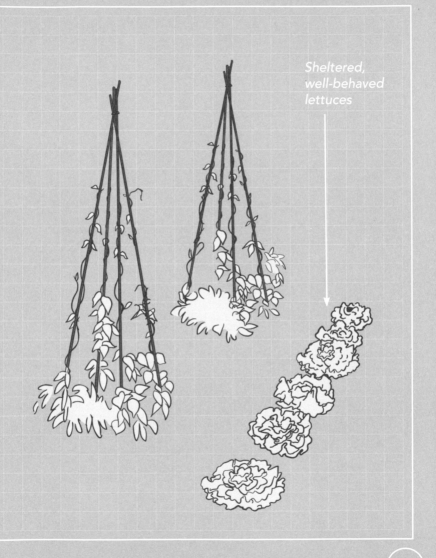

Sheltered, well-behaved lettuces

POOR-SOIL PLANT BONANZA

If part of your garden is drier than the Mojave Desert in a heat wave and you've been struggling to get flowers to grow in it for years, don't despair. You can turn your sandy soil conditions into a bonus and plant a Mediterranean herb garden there instead.

Herbs such as rosemary, thyme, sage and oregano flourish in poor soil and hot conditions, so plant these in your nutrient-deprived patch rather than trying to alter the natural condition of your soil. You'll have a successful crop of plants with very little effort – and some tasty herbs to spice up your cooking too.

Healthy herbs

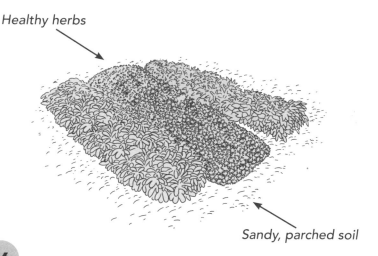

Sandy, parched soil

PEST-CONTROL HACKS

Gardeners have been doing battle with pests since time immemorial, so we've gathered all the best nuggets of pest-control wisdom into one place – this chapter of pest-control hacks. Find out how to deter mozzies, save your black beans from aphid attack and discourage some ants into the bargain. Who says gardening isn't fun?!

CD BIRD-SCARER

Here's a great hack for keeping birds away from your vegetable patch, and all you need are some old CDs and a few lengths of string.

If you don't have a shelf of CDs gathering dust at home, pick some up in a charity shop. Tie several CDs to one length of string. Hang your musical mobile next to your veggie patch, in the branches of a tree or from a fence. The light reflected by the shiny discs will scare off the birds, even if your choice of music doesn't.

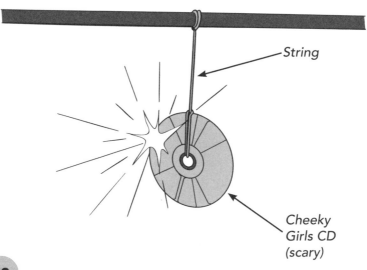

String

Cheeky
Girls CD
(scary)

BAKING-SODA ANT TRAP

When ants invade your patio, it can be hard to get rid of them – they don't turn up in small numbers, but bring all their friends to the party, too. Here's an easy way to oust these prevalent pests.

Mix one tablespoon of icing sugar with a tablespoon of baking soda and place in a jam-jar lid in your ant-infested area. The icing sugar will attract the ants, and the baking soda is your active ingredient, which will put an end to their picnic-pestering plans – and indeed any other plans they might have been making.

Icing-sugar bait

Baking soda – boom!

Your finished anti-ant powder

BRIDAL BERRY PROTECTION

If there's one sure way to stop birds from decimating your berry crops it's by putting up some netting, but if you haven't got the time or money to invest in complicated frames or cages try this hack instead.

Get hold of a length of wedding net fabric (easily found online) and drape it over your berry bushes. Secure with strategically placed clothes pegs and you can be sure that it'll be *you* enjoying a berry bounty – not the birds. Now all you need is a bowl of cream!

Bridal barrier (hides blooming berries as well as blushing brides)

Clothes peg

Your blueberries – untouched by greedy beaks

BLACK-FLY BEAN SAVER

Black-fly are even more fond of your bean crops than you are, but this simple hack will stop them in their tracks – and you don't even need to mix up a magic potion to do it.

Black-fly will only target the growing tips of your bean plants, so if you spot them, just pinch off the tips and discard. The flies won't fancy the older growth and will be gone for good. Easy!

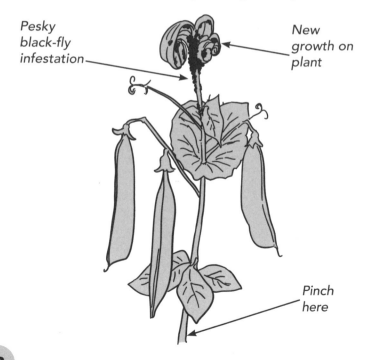

Pesky black-fly infestation

New growth on plant

Pinch here

CITRUS SLUG SORTER

Slugs are, without a doubt, the arch enemy of all gardeners, but if salting or skewering the slimy critters is not for you, why not tempt them away from your prize lettuces with this handy hack?

Slugs are looking for an easy source of food and shelter, so scoop out an orange and place the empty skin upside down in your garden, at a safe distance from your prized plants. The slugs will be attracted to this fruity B&B instead. Simply gather them up and remove them in the morning.

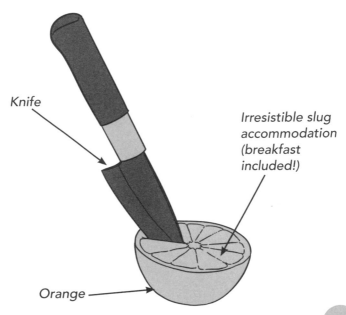

Knife

Irresistible slug accommodation (breakfast included!)

Orange

SLIPPERY-POLE CAT DETERRENT

One of the joys of having a garden is watching the comings and goings of our feathery friends, but birds aren't the only creatures who see a bird table as a good place to stock up on supplies – and it's not the birdseed that next door's cat is salivating over!

Stop cats from climbing to takeaway heaven by applying a layer of petroleum jelly to the pole of your bird table. The grease will stop sneaky feline predators from getting a grip on the pole and your feathery friends can come and go without fearing for their lives.

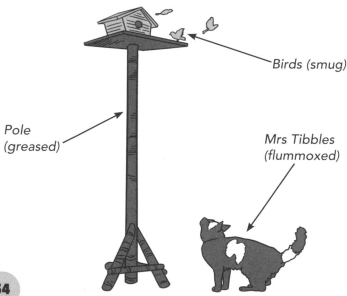

Birds (smug)

Pole (greased)

Mrs Tibbles (flummoxed)

MOVE THOSE MOZZIES

There's nothing worse than hearing the irritating buzz of a mosquito as you're enjoying a well-earned rest on the patio, but there's an easy way to get rid of these pesky pests without resorting to sprays or over-energetic swatting.

Mosquitos hate the scent of lavender, so position pots of this fragrant plant around your seating area and you can relax without getting bitten to pieces by the little buzzing blighters. Rosemary, basil or garlic will work too, so you can get rid of the bugs and bag a bountiful harvest at the same time. Brilliant!

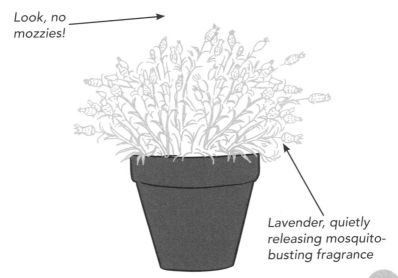

Look, no mozzies!

Lavender, quietly releasing mosquito-busting fragrance

APHID SPRAY-AWAY

If your plants are overrun with aphids it can be tempting to head to the garden centre and stock up on pesticide, but there's a much easier, cheaper solution you can mix up at home.

Simply stir a teaspoon of baking soda into 100 millilitres of cooking oil. Add a couple of teaspoons of this mixture to a cup of water and pour into a clean plant-spray bottle. Spray your affected plants with this once every few days and the offending creatures will soon disappear.

Tasteful gardening gloves (optional)

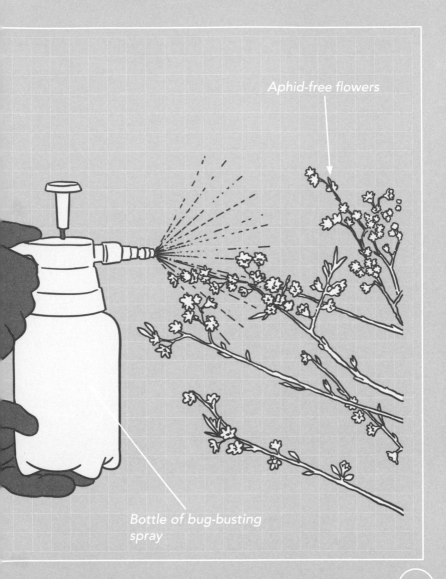

Aphid-free flowers

Bottle of bug-busting spray

COPPER-TAPE PLANT DEFENDER

This simple hack will stop slugs and snails from targeting your favourite pot plants.

Since these slimy customers are repelled by copper, a ring of copper tape applied around the rim of a plant pot will stop them from climbing in and devouring your delphiniums. (The metal gives the garden pests a low-level electric shock.) Find the tape in your local garden centre (or online). Find the slugs in your garden… but not for long!

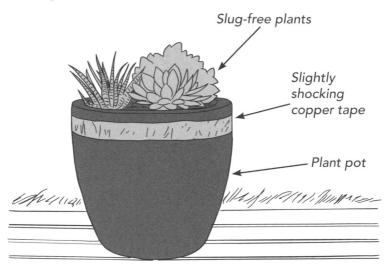

Slug-free plants

Slightly shocking copper tape

Plant pot

CUTLERY PATCH PROTECTOR

A lot of hard work goes into preparing the perfect planting patch, so the last thing you want is the neighbouring moggies pooping in it once you've finished hoeing. Use this easy hack to keep toileting cats at bay.

Break up any areas of finely tilled soil between seedlings by sticking plastic cutlery into the ground at intervals among your plants. If next door's felines can't find a suitable space to dig, they'll have to build their latrine elsewhere!

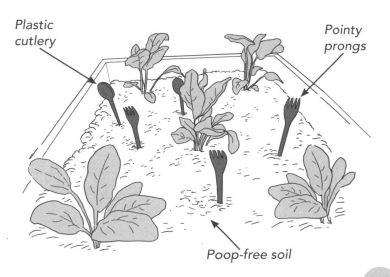

Plastic cutlery

Pointy prongs

Poop-free soil

CRAFTY COMPANIONS

Here's a clever trick to get rid of carrot-root fly and keep your crop healthy.

Plant spring onions in among your carrots. The smell of onions will deter carrot-root fly. Even better, the smell of carrots will get rid of onion fly, so the crops protect one another. Two hacks for the price of one! (Extra tip: mint is another aromatic crop that acts as an aphid deterrent, but remember to contain it in pots or it can run wild and take over your plot.)

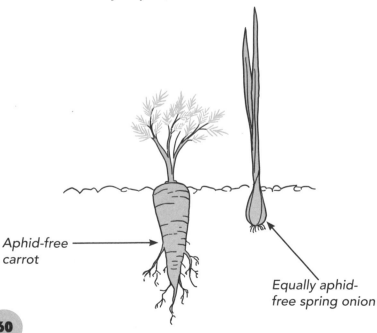

Aphid-free carrot

Equally aphid-free spring onion

VEGGIE-PATCH HACKS

The veggie patch is where you can reap the rewards of all your spade-work, with juicy tomatoes, earthy spuds and more raspberries than you can shake a cane at. Read on for some easy ways to make sure your produce is tasty and well tended. We've even included some ideas for what to do with it all afterwards! (As a general guide, springtime is the season to plant your produce, which you can harvest over the summer and autumn, but do check seasonal info on your plant packaging.)

BUCKET POTATOES

Potatoes are the hippies of the vegetable world – they're happy to put down roots anywhere – so try this hack for a tasty crop of spuds on your doorstep.

Leave some seed potatoes to chit – yes, very funny! – for a couple of weeks. Once they've developed shoots, drill drainage holes in the bottom of a large plastic bucket and half-fill with compost. Pop in three or so spuds and carefully cover with soil. As they grow, mound up soil around their stems and water once a week. Your harvest is ready when the plants flower and turn yellow. Easy!

Sprouted potatoes

Large bucket
(potatoes' ideal home)

TOMATO-SLICE SEED STARTER

If you've got an over-ripe tomato languishing in your fridge, don't throw it out – turn it into a tomato nursery instead.

Slice the top and bottom off the squishy fruit and plant the remaining slice in a pot, sliced-side up, covering it thinly with earth. The seeds will have plenty of nourishment from the surrounding fruit as they start to grow, and will simply need thinning out and potting on when they're large enough. You'll end up with a bumper harvest of toms without having to shell out on seedlings!

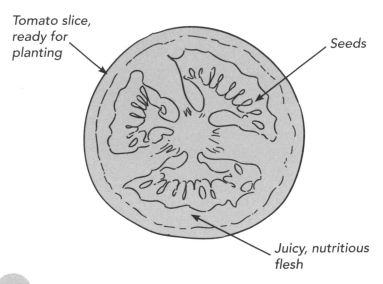

Tomato slice, ready for planting

Seeds

Juicy, nutritious flesh

NETTLE COMPOST QUICKENER

Making your own compost is one of the greenest things a gardener can do. Not only are you putting your fruit and veg peelings, tea bags and garden clippings to good use, but it's a use that helps you grow more plants – and earn extra smug points! But making compost takes time, so here's a tip to get you speedier results.

Nettles naturally speed up the decomposition process, so add some to your compost bin and mix in. Pick younger nettles, chop them up and add them, but don't include the root, which takes longer to break down. Even nettles have their uses!

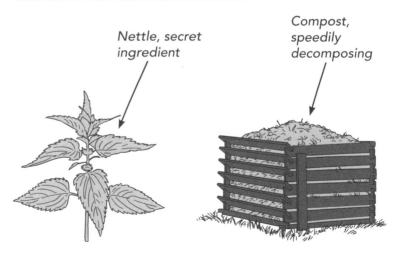

Nettle, secret ingredient

Compost, speedily decomposing

CAULIFLOWER COVER-UP

If you're a fan of cauliflowers – and you don't mind eating a vegetable that looks like an enormous white brain – this is a great trick to keep your crops' curds bright until you're ready to harvest.

Cauliflowers turn yellow when they're exposed to too much sunlight, but luckily the plants come with a built-in shade device to hand. Just draw together two or three of the surrounding leaves around the cauliflower head and secure at the top with a clothes peg. Beautifully blanched veg with no effort at all! (Bleurgh!)

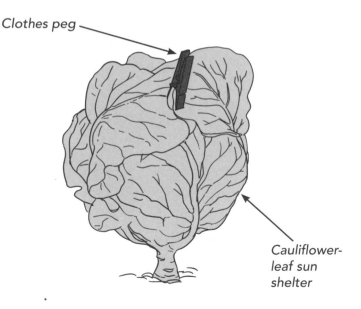

Clothes peg

Cauliflower-leaf sun shelter

EPSOM SALTS TOMATO SWEETENER

Here's a great way to boost the size and flavour of your tomatoes.

Tomato plants need lots of magnesium – which is one of the main components in Epsom salts. If you mix one tablespoon of Epsom salt into a gallon (4.5 litres) of water and use this to water your plants every three weeks, you'll notice they will produce a bumper crop and they'll taste sweeter too. (When transplanting plants, you can scatter a tablespoon of Epsom salts into the soil beneath – but not touching – their roots for a similar effect.)

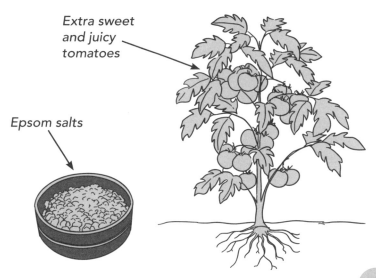

Extra sweet and juicy tomatoes

Epsom salts

HANDY HERB-CUBES HACK

This tip is great for preserving herbs, so that you have a supply all year round. It even saves you time in the kitchen, too!

Chop up soft-leaved herbs (basil, oregano, parsley, etc.) and freeze them in ice-cube trays topped up with water. Once frozen, you can store your cubes in marked freezer bags and easily grab a cube or two to add directly to soups or casseroles whenever needed. (A herby ice cube makes a great addition to your favourite cocktail too – so have fun experimenting!)

Fresh herbs, frozen and flavoursome

Ice cubes, ready to pop into drink

SPEEDY RADISH ROW-MARKER

If you have trouble remembering where you've planted your rows of slower-growing veg, how about mixing in a speedy grower to help you keep track?

For example, if you put in a radish seed every now and then among your line of parsnips, you'll have handy green reminders popping up within just a few days to mark your row. The radishes will be ready for picking long before the parsnips have fully developed, so you'll get two crops in the space of one.

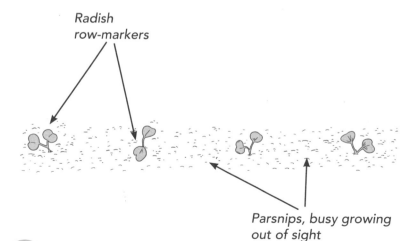

Radish
row-markers

Parsnips, busy growing
out of sight

STRAWBERRY HANGING BASKETS

Strawberries are a great addition to your kitchen garden – for obvious reasons – but they can be so keen to reproduce that they'll send out runners all over the place and end up taking over your entire vegetable patch.

Keep your berries contained by growing them in hanging baskets – three to four plants per basket should do the trick. They'll look beautiful and you'll enjoy the benefits of a boosted harvest too, as keeping the berries up off the ground discourages pests and diseases. All you need to add is the Pimm's.

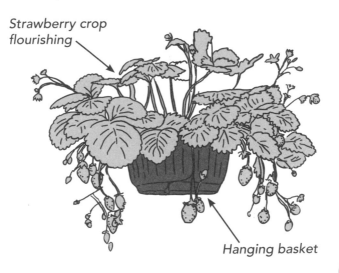

Strawberry crop flourishing

Hanging basket

STOCKING ONION STORE

Your onion crop is ready and you've got dozens of the blighters to store - so where do you put them? Hang them in some tights of course!

If you want your harvest to last, you need to dry out your crop and store them somewhere cool and dry, so hanging them in your shed knotted in some nylons is the perfect answer. (Don't put in any bruised or blemished bulbs or they'll go bad.) Whether you choose a pair of understated nude tights or racy lacy stockings is up to you.

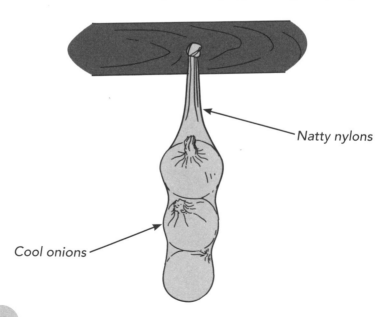

Natty nylons

Cool onions

PEPPER PINCH-OUT

Peppers are great to grow: you can plant them in pots and move them about to get the best of the sun and – even better – they look impressive when fruit starts to develop. If you want to harvest bigger peppers from your plants, this super-easy tip is for you.

When your plants first blossom, pinch off those early flowers. Rather than producing a few smaller peppers right away, your plant will put its energy into growing bigger and giving you a higher yield of larger peppers later in the season. You'll be frantically searching for 'pepper recipes' before the year is out!

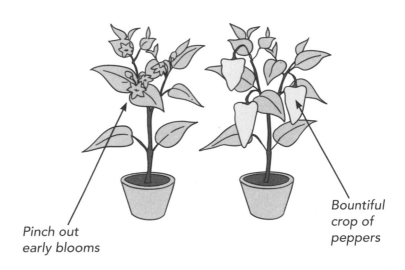

Pinch out early blooms

Bountiful crop of peppers

SHOE-ORGANISER HERB GARDEN

Vertical gardening is all the rage, so get in on the act with a canvas shoe organiser and a curtain pole – obviously!

Fasten the curtain rail to a suitable wall – remember, it will need to support the weight of your vertical garden. Hang the shoe organiser from it and check that the pockets drain when watered – make a couple of holes in each if not – then fill them with compost to 3 cm below the top. Add seeds or herbs and miniature tomato plants and enjoy your vertical harvest.

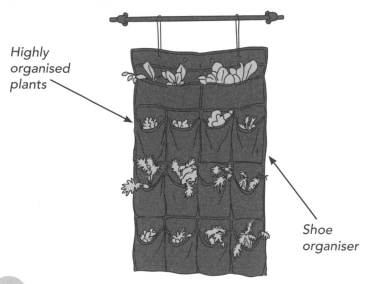

Highly organised plants

Shoe organiser

TREE AND BUSH HACKS

If you've invested in a new tree, you'll want to make sure your precious purchase flourishes, so here are a host of hacks for settling your tree in, as well as looking after established old-timers. And as for the heaps of leaves these majestic seasonal plants thoughtlessly scatter all over your lawn once a year... there's a hack for those too.

TREE ANCHORAGE HACK

If you've bought a new tree, don't just dig a hole and drop it in when you get home – your tree won't be able to establish a decent root system. Here's how to make sure your ace acer doesn't keel over as soon as there's a bit of a breeze.

When prepping the ground for your tree, dig over an area that is at least three times the width of the container it's currently in. Remove any stones from this tree zone, then dig your planting hole. Your tree's roots will be able to establish themselves deeply in the surrounding soil and it will be safe whatever the weather.

New tree, permanently upright

Well-prepped soil

Clever
gardener

QUICK PICKING TIP

So your apple trees are groaning with fruit, but how can you pick your harvest quickly without climbing a rickety ladder and painstakingly plucking individual apples?

Easy! All you need is a few friends and an old sheet. Get your pals to hold the sheet between them beneath a bountiful branch and give the branch a good shake. The fruit will drop safely into the sheet, saving you time and effort. (The fun factor is an added bonus.)

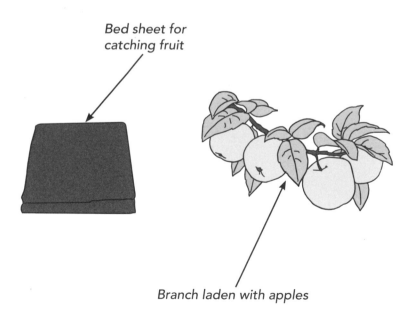

Bed sheet for catching fruit

Branch laden with apples

CANE-PLANTING GUIDE

The quickest way to kill off a newly bought tree is to plant it too deeply, so avoid accidental 'arbicide' and dig a hole that's exactly the same depth as the root ball of your tree.

Now take a look at the nursery soil line at the base of the tree's trunk. Place a cane across your hole and make sure that, when your tree is in situ, the nursery line matches the height of the cane or is slightly above it. Any deeper and your tree will be in trouble.

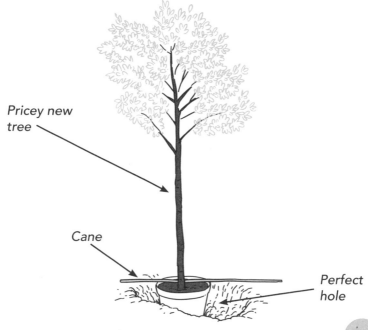

Pricey new tree

Cane

Perfect hole

HORIZONTAL HEDGE TRIM

Formal hedges look great with their crisp straight lines, but if you are cutting by eye a trimming error will stand out a mile. Here's a way to make sure your hedge is perfect without getting the spirit level out.

Before you even plug in your hedge trimmer (or get out the loppers and elbow grease), push a garden cane into the ground at either end of your hedge and stretch a piece of string taut between the canes. Make sure the string is tied at the same height on each cane, then use it as a cutting guide to avoid creating a topiary ski slope.

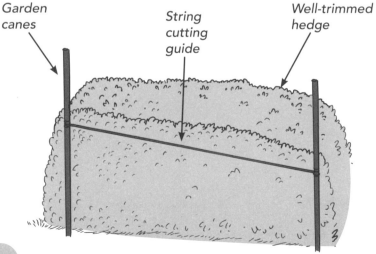

Garden canes

String cutting guide

Well-trimmed hedge

ORNAMENTAL GRASS RETAINER

Ornamental grasses are useful plants: they soften the edges of your beds, link plants that would otherwise clash side-by-side and can even hide that unsightly corner of your garden – you know the one I mean! But how can you prevent these often vigorous growers from rampaging out of the flower bed, across your lawn and – quite possibly – taking over the rest of the planet?

Simply sink a row of old roof slates around the edge of their territory and you'll have your ornamental beauties corralled in one place, no problem.

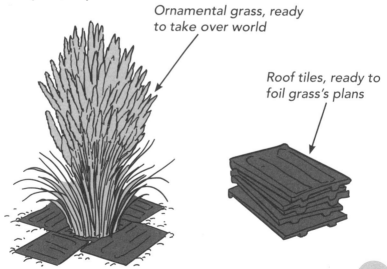

Ornamental grass, ready to take over world

Roof tiles, ready to foil grass's plans

COOL CUTTING TRICK

The best way to propagate your favourite tree or shrub is from a cutting, but as soon as you separate your baby plant from its parent, it's a race against time to get it settled into a pot and ready to root without drying out.

If you wrap your cuttings in damp paper towels and put them straight into a plastic bag as soon as you clip them off, you'll minimise evaporation and give them the best chance of survival. Pot up as soon as possible with a little rooting hormone on the cutting tip and you'll have little arboreal offspring in no time.

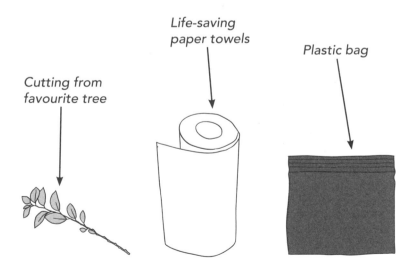

Cutting from favourite tree

Life-saving paper towels

Plastic bag

SPEEDY CHERRY SNIP

A tree full of cherries is a delight to behold, but picking those tasty fruit one-by-one sure is time-consuming (and ripping each fruit off its stalk can result in some messy collateral damage).

Save time – and cherries – by snipping through several stalks at once with a sharp pair of scissors. (If you cut the cherries above a small container, they'll drop into it without harm.) Your harvest time will be dramatically reduced, leaving you more time to work out what to do with all those darn cherries!

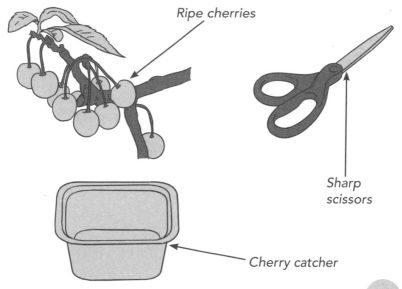

Ripe cherries

Sharp scissors

Cherry catcher

EASY PRUNING (1, 2, 3)

Fruit trees need a good prune once a year, but how do you know what to cut away? There's no great mystery, just wait until the leaves have dropped (so you can see what you're doing) and keep it simple with these three steps:

1. Cut away any branches that are broken or diseased.
2. Lop off any branches that cross or rub against others.
3. Prune any branches that grow straight up or down. (They won't bear much fruit.)

You'll end up with healthy, well-spaced branches growing at 45 to 60 degrees out from the trunk. Great work!

Vertical branches – lop these off

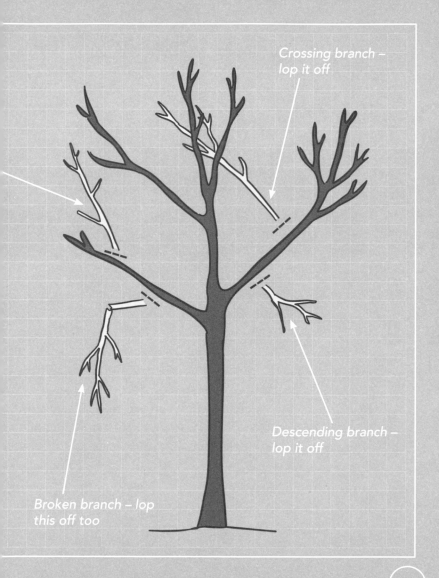

Crossing branch –
lop it off

Descending branch –
lop it off

Broken branch – lop
this off too

DIY DRIED FRUIT

If you often end up with a glut of fruit, drying it is a nutritious alternative to making tonnes of jam – here's how.

Preheat the oven to 140°F (60°C). Clean the fruit and remove cores, skins, stalks, etc. Chop into slices and dunk them in some orange juice before laying them out on baking sheets sprayed with non-stick spray. Put in the oven until dehydrated (this can take six to eight hours). Put the finished fruit into jars, but leave unsealed for five days until all traces of moisture have evaporated. Store in a cool, dry place and your dried fruit will last for six months to a year.

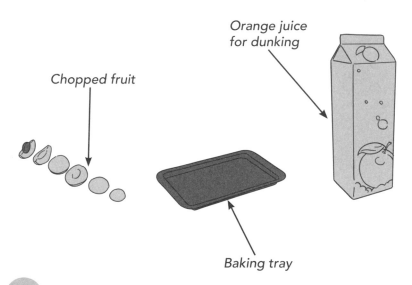

Orange juice for dunking

Chopped fruit

Baking tray

LEAF-MOULD SOIL CONDITIONER

If you're up to your ears in fallen leaves come autumn time, here's a great way to put them to use. (The leaves, not your ears.)

Rake up the leaves and pop them into a bin bag, moisten and pierce holes in the bag for air flow. Check every couple of weeks to make sure the leaves are still moist. After six months to a year you'll have your finished product – leaf mould. It's a great conditioner for soil and will improve its water retention, so dig leaf mould into your beds or add it to containers.

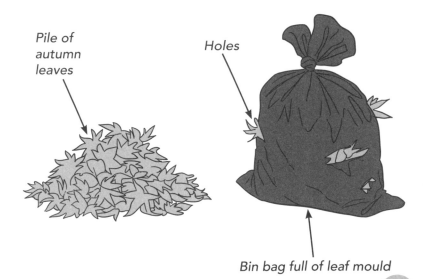

Pile of autumn leaves

Holes

Bin bag full of leaf mould

GARDEN-DECORATION HACKS

These brilliant hacks will add a touch of colour and style to your garden. Why call in a garden designer when you can make your own coastal corner, build a quirky bench from breeze blocks and brighten up your patio with some speedy paving-stone painting? And then, after lunch, you can just sit back, relax and enjoy the gentle tinkling of your door key wind chime.

UPCYCLED CHAIR PLANTER

You can make a hole in just about anything and turn it into a planter, so why not fire up the jigsaw and put an old chair out of its misery?

Cut a hole in the seat to fit your container. For a smart look, rub down and prime before painting in a bright colour. (If that sounds like hard work, remind yourself that the distressed look also works well and leave as is.) Plant up with more bold colours and a bit of trailing greenery at the front (to stop your hot seat from looking too much like a commode).

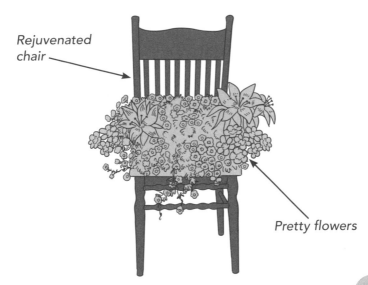

Rejuvenated chair

Pretty flowers

PLANT-POT LIGHTHOUSE

Like many of us, solar stick lights look more attractive by night, but here's a way to make them look good during daylight hours too.

Buy three or four terracotta pots of different sizes (ones with fairly big drainage holes in the bottom) that will stack on top of one another to form a stack that resembles a lighthouse. Paint the pots with primer, then decorate in appropriate colours, adding details such as windows with a paint pen. Glue your pots in place and pop the solar light into the hole at the top. Scatter some pebbles at the base for a natty nautical look.

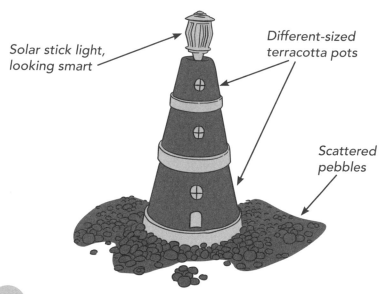

Solar stick light, looking smart

Different-sized terracotta pots

Scattered pebbles

MAGICAL MIRROR HACK

Hanging a mirror in your garden can make it look twice as big – as well as giving you the chance to check your hair while outside. So why not try hanging one?

A round mirror looks like a window, while a full-length mirror with a few paving stones leading up to it can look like a gateway into a secret garden. Make sure your mirror is well hung (ahem) and tilt if necessary to reflect lovely green foliage (rather than your bins). Make sure your mirror isn't in direct sunlight and avoid any avian accidents by not hanging it too high.

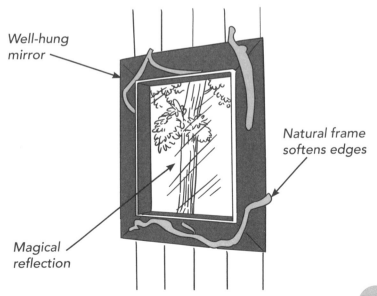

Well-hung mirror

Natural frame softens edges

Magical reflection

QUICK COASTAL CORNER

You don't need to re-sculpt every inch of your garden to give it a new look. A nautical corner adds character with very little effort. (Phew!)

Plant your corner with some grasses and sea holly, then mulch with gravel. Decorate with pebbles, seashells, the odd starfish, driftwood… take a coastal walk and bring back some décor from your trip. (Check online to make sure your local beach is OK with this.) If the sea air has really gone to your head, you could even add rope edging, a cheerfully painted fence and a bubbling water feature to bring you the sound of the sea. Now just pull up a deckchair.

Grasses

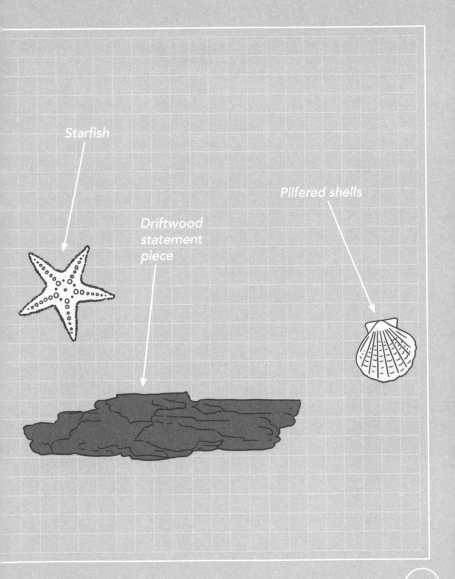

Starfish

Driftwood statement piece

Pilfered shells

TIN-CAN LANTERNS

Tin-can lanterns look great on a path or patio – and a punched-out letter design allows lots of potential for spelling out amusing words.

Remove the tin's label and rinse out. Fill with uncooked rice, top up with water and freeze to make punching the holes easier. Make a template for your design and tape it around the can. Fold a towel and nestle your tin into it, so that it doesn't slide around. Next, use a hammer and nail to carefully punch your design into the can. Defrost in warm water to remove the rice and pop in a tea light. More beans, anyone?

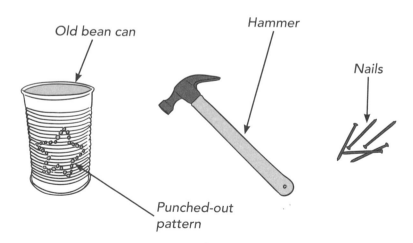

Old bean can

Hammer

Nails

Punched-out
pattern

PAINTED-STONE PLANT MARKERS

If you're looking for a way to label your plants without resorting to scrawling something on a broken piece of yogurt pot, look no further. These plant markers will stay put and look good too.

For each label, paint a smooth stone with acrylic paint for a background colour. If you're labelling veggies and feeling artistic, how about decorating each in the shape of the vegetable you're labelling? Once dry, add details such as lettering, and seal with a coat of clear varnish.

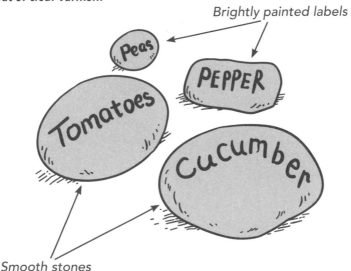

Brightly painted labels

Smooth stones

BRIGHT BLOCK BENCH

Imagine how proud you'll feel once you've made your own bench from 12 breeze blocks and four 10-foot pieces of 4-inch by 4-inch wood. Time to make your dream come true…

Assemble the first side of your bench with four breeze blocks set vertically side-by-side and another two balanced horizontally across the top. Position the second side about 3 metres away and fix all the blocks together using concrete adhesive. When dry, paint them with masonry paint (a couple of tester pots will do the trick) and slide the wood into place and fix with more adhesive. Cover with outdoor cushions and test your new bench extensively whenever possible.

Brightly painted breeze blocks

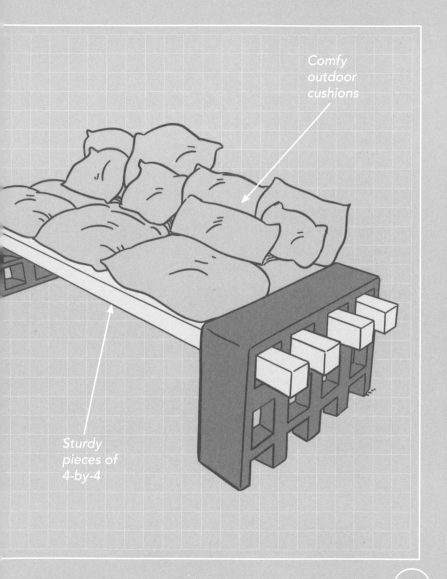

Comfy outdoor cushions

Sturdy pieces of 4-by-4

PUNCHY PATIO PAINTING

If your patio starts to look a little tired and grey – and let's face it, most patios do – here's a quick way of giving it a lift without re-laying any slabs.

If your tiles are really grimy, borrow a pressure washer and blast everything clean. Pick out a few 'random' tiles, prime them and then paint in bold contrasting colours (they will need a couple of coats at least). Then finish with a sealant for a long-lasting, cheerful burst of colour that will brighten your garden all year round!

Patio with new lease of life

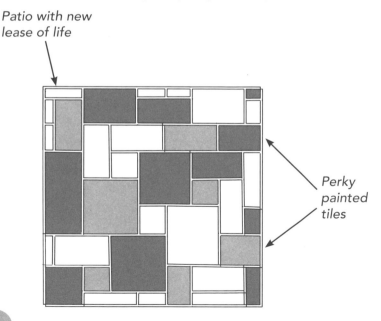

Perky painted tiles

WELLIE-BOOT HANGING GARDEN

The good thing about wellie boots – apart from the fact that they keep your feet dry – is that they come in so many colourful designs. This hack shows you how to turn cheap and cheerful wellies into a statement hanging garden.

Start by drilling a couple of drainage holes in the bottom of each boot. (You'll need another hole at the back, too, about 3 cm below the top, for hanging.) Fill your boots with compost and plant up with flowers that will contrast nicely with your colour scheme. Hang on your fence with cup hooks. Boot-iful!

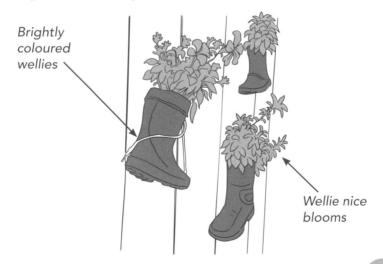

Brightly coloured wellies

Wellie nice blooms

DOOR-KEY WIND CHIME

Wind chimes can be made out of anything from seashells to old cutlery. They look quirky, sound beautiful – and cost next to nothing to make. For an easy wind chime (no drilling involved!) gather together any old keys you no longer use. Paint them with acrylic paints for a colourful look. Suspend the keys at intervals along a sturdy stick using equal lengths of string, hang above your patio and enjoy the sound of the wind in the keys.

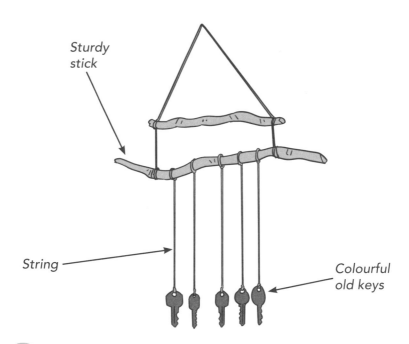

Sturdy stick

String

Colourful old keys

WILD FLOWER HACKS

Wild flowers are low-maintenance and look great, so here are a host of hacks to help you introduce them to your garden. Whether you want to create your own quick-and-easy meadow or a woodland corner, you'll find everything you need to know in the following pages. Plus – free seeds, anyone? It would be rude not to.

FREE SEEDS HACKS

If you're looking for free wild flower seeds that will flourish in your garden, take a walk in a local meadow. It's illegal to dig up wild plants (obviously!) but you *can* gather your own seeds (with the landowner's permission). Here's how:

1. Photograph the plants while in flower so you'll recognise them, then…
2. … return when the seed heads are dry, and clip off a few, putting each in a paper bag.
3. Give each bag a shake to loosen the seeds. Remove any debris.
4. Dry out your seeds and label ready for planting!

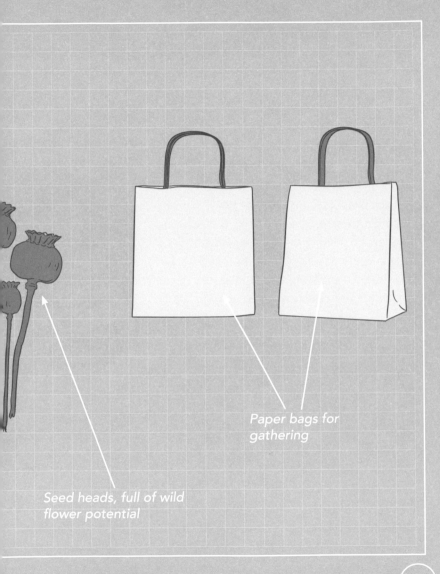

Paper bags for
gathering

Seed heads, full of wild
flower potential

SPEEDY WILD FLOWER MEADOW

Turn your lawn into a beautiful wild flower meadow and you'll only have to mow the blooming thing once a year!

While you *can* plant your meadow from seed why not save time and see instant results with some wild flower plugs instead? (You can order these online.) Dig a plug-sized hole for each, pop a little compost in the bottom and loosen the edges for roots to establish. Plug in your baby plants and you're off! (For even speedier results, roll out the ready-sown wild flower turf, but be warned – it doesn't come cheap!)

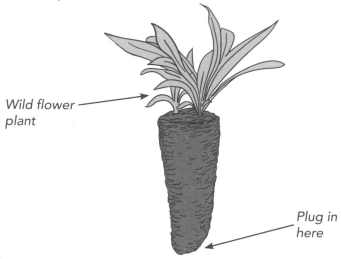

Wild flower plant

Plug in here

COFFEE-TIN SEED SPREADER

So you're sowing a wild flower lawn from scratch. Your seed pack tells you how much seed you need. You mix it in with some sand to make the job easier, and then you take a quick coffee break to recover.

At this point you *could* go out and buy a fancy seed spreader, but stop! You can make your own from that empty coffee tin. Just turn it upside down, make a couple of lines of small holes in the base with a hammer and nail and you're ready to sow.

Yikes, you're out of coffee!

Nail

Hammer

YELLOW-RATTLE GRASS ZAPPER

It's survival of the fittest out there on the lawn, but this handy hack will help your wild flowers establish themselves.

They'll be competing with the grass around them for nutrients from day one, but including yellow rattle seeds in the mix will give them an advantage. When yellow rattle grows, it taps into the roots of surrounding grasses to get the nutrients it needs, so it will weaken established grass allowing your wildflowers to take hold. Sneaky, but useful!

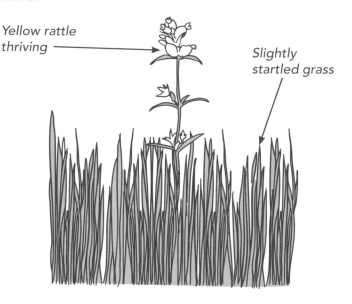

Yellow rattle thriving

Slightly startled grass

WILD (BUT ELEGANT) PLANTING PLAN

The unkempt meadow look may not be for you, but you can still include wild flowers in your garden without it looking like the filming location for a hay-fever tablet advert. Here's how to bring a touch of class to your planting.

Pick a single colour for your wild flowers to contrast with the foliage in your garden. White (white campion or lily of the valley) or blue (cornflowers or harebells) both work well. Add some structure by pruning your evergreens into bold shapes and your garden will look like it belongs at Chelsea (Flower Show, not Stamford Bridge). Who said wild had to be unruly?

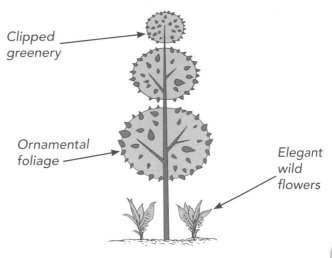

Clipped greenery

Ornamental foliage

Elegant wild flowers

MASON-JAR SOIL TEST

Some wild flowers thrive in sandy soil, others suit silt or clay. Check your soil type with this easy test.

Half-fill a mason jar with soil, add water until three-quarters full, then add a teaspoon of washing-up liquid. Put the lid on, give the jar a shake and leave to settle into layers. The bottom layer is sand; the next, silt and the top, clay. The perfect combination is 20 per cent clay, 40 per cent silt and 40 per cent sand, so compare your soil to this to see what conditions you can offer your wild beauties.

Mucky water

Organic bits and bobs

Clay

Silt

Sand

SANDPAPER SCARIFIER

This hack shows you how to speed up the germination of any hard-coated wild flower seeds you're planning on planting. Scarifying the seeds – breaking down their tough coatings – makes it much more likely that they'll germinate and it's satisfying to do, too.

Sandwich a handful of seeds between two sheets of sandpaper and rub firmly until you hear the outer cases beginning to crack. Don't push too hard. When the cases have been breached and you can see a little of the green beneath peeking through, they're ready for planting.

Two pieces of scarifying sandpaper

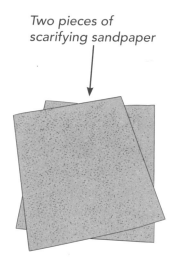

Wild flower seeds, tough ones to crack!

PAPER-TOWEL GERMINATION CHEAT

If you think that the cold, damp months of winter are only good for pre-booking summer holidays, think again. Many wild flower seeds need this miserable weather to germinate. Cunning gardeners can mimic this overwintering to get their stored seeds ready to plant. Here's how you can join their ranks.

Soak your seeds overnight, then dampen some paper towels and lay them out flat. Sprinkle the seeds on one half of each paper towel and then fold over to hold in place. Slide into a sandwich bag and keep in the fridge for a month. After this, check regularly – your seeds should germinate after about eight weeks.

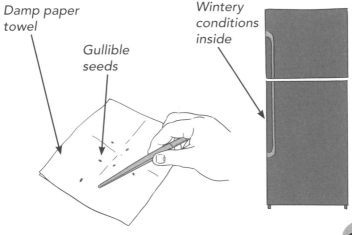

Damp paper towel

Gullible seeds

Wintery conditions inside

WILD FLOWER TYRE PLANTER

Hmm, sowing wild flower seeds in a planter made from an old tyre… On one hand, it's a statement about nature reclaiming the planet after humankind has over-cultivated it. And on the other, it looks pretty darn smart.

First, with the tyre lying flat, cut some drainage holes in the 'bottom' (the inside of the rim nearest to the ground). Now, let your creative juices flow and paint your tyre (spray paint is a good option here). Finish by planting it up with a not-too-rich mixture of compost and your own garden soil, plus wild flower seeds, of course!

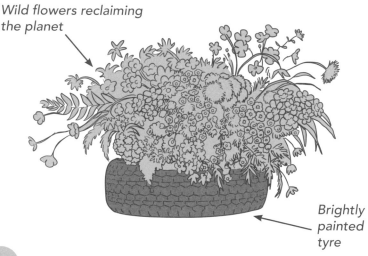

Wild flowers reclaiming the planet

Brightly painted tyre

WOODLAND BULB BONANZA

Woodland bulbs make an easy wild flower border – snowdrops, bluebells and anemones all flourish in the shade, need zero attention and reward your inactivity with bright patches of colour in the spring. But did you know that your bulbs are busy growing babies underground? Here's how to benefit from this subterranean bulb bonanza and stop your flowers from becoming too congested.

When your plants have finished flowering, dig up the bulbs. Break off any new bulbs and plant out (if sturdy), transfer to pots (if small) or store until the autumn. Your new bulbs can brighten up another corner of your garden or will make great gifts for your green-fingered friends. Return the parent bulbs to the ground for another year's woodland magic.

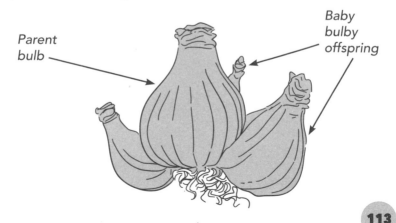

Parent bulb

Baby bulby offspring

WEEDING HACKS

If there's one thing that unites us gardeners it's the eternal battle against a universal enemy: weeds. They're tenacious little blighters and – while nothing will rid your patch of weeds forever – we can certainly put up a good fight. So here are some cunning tips for defeating our little green nemeses without reaching for pricey weedkiller or putting in too much hard labour. Into battle!

BOIL THEM!

This is a really effective method for exterminating individual weeds that spring up through paving stones – and all you have to do is boil the kettle.

Pour boiling water on each weed for speedy weed-killing results. It works well on younger plants as the water can penetrate all the way to the root, so try to zap them before they get too out of hand. Easy – and you might as well make yourself a cuppa while the kettle's on.

Kettle full of boiling water

Evil weed

RULE THEM OUT!

This tip works well for weeds with deep taproots, such as dandelions. You can't just yank these persistent pests up by the foliage – well, you can, but they'll spring up again as long as their root stays in the ground. You need a cunning secret weapon in your arsenal: you need… a ruler!

Get a steel ruler (or a tent stake) and push it into the ground next to your stubborn weed. Do this in a circle around your weed and then pull it up, root and all. Another problem solved!

Dandelion

Devilish root

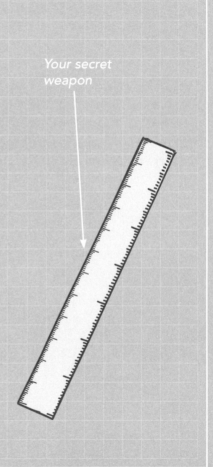

Your secret weapon

117

DISSOLVE THEM!

Maybe you've got a larger patch of stubborn weeds and boiling water won't do the trick? Don't worry – you can go into battle with another household substance: vinegar.

Stir a little salt into a cup of white vinegar, add a squeeze of washing-up liquid (to help it stick to the weeds) and mix. Put into a spray bottle and spray the leaves of your offending weeds. (Vinegar is acidic and will break down the cell membranes of the plant.) Just take care not to spray any plants you want to keep.

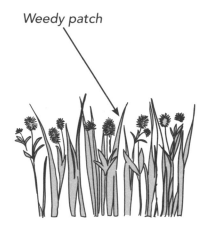

Weedy patch

Spray bottle

Salt 'n' vinegar – not just for chips!

SMOTHER THEM!

Here's a great hack for de-weeding an entire flower bed in one go – and, even better, you'll improve the soil quality at the same time.

First, water your weed-ridden flower bed, then cover the area with overlapping sheets of newspaper. Water again to keep the paper in place, then add a good layer of mulch (shredded leaves or bark chips are perfect). Now sit back and wait! The paper will not only kill off your weeds, but will decompose and improve the health of your soil. What's not to love?

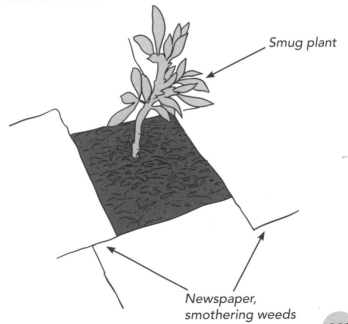

Smug plant

Newspaper, smothering weeds

DECAPITATE THEM!

The secret to keeping your garden weed-free is to 'weed them before you see them'. The best way to do this is with a hoe, so here's a hot hoeing tip:

Always hoe on a dry day, never when it has been raining. Go over your patch – beheading the little green invaders before they get a chance to establish – and then leave the weeds on the surface of the soil to dry out. (If the soil is damp, they can re-root and – like the baddy at the end of a horror movie – resurrect themselves.)

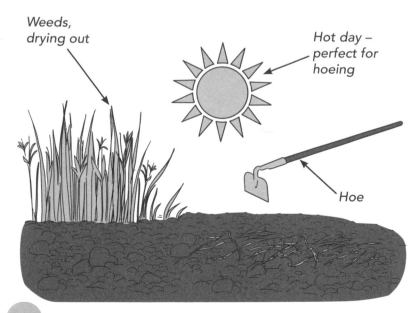

Weeds, drying out

Hot day – perfect for hoeing

Hoe

DEHYDRATE THEM!

It's simple to deal with weeds that pop up through cracks in your driveway. Just dampen the offending weeds and pour salt onto them – they'll soon wither and die as the salt dries out the leaves and stems. For really stubborn weeds, cut their tops off before treating with salt. (Remember salt will kill off other plants, too, so this method is best saved for isolated weed growth.)

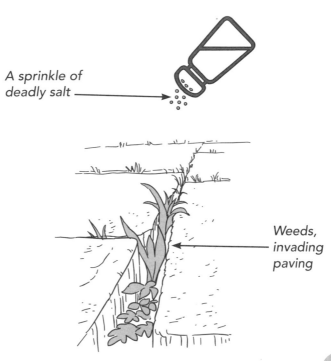

A sprinkle of deadly salt

Weeds, invading paving

BURN THEM!

Here's a great way of zapping individual weeds, as well as getting rid of tufts of grass in tough-to-access cracks and spaces – BURN THEM!

While you will need to invest in a suitable blowtorch for this hack, they aren't too pricey and using them is very satisfying if you've had a tough day. Just fire it up, point it at the evil weed and burn it to kingdom come. (Note: do take care to read the operating instructions, and don't use the blowtorch against a flammable surface.)

Soon-to-be-extra-crispy weed

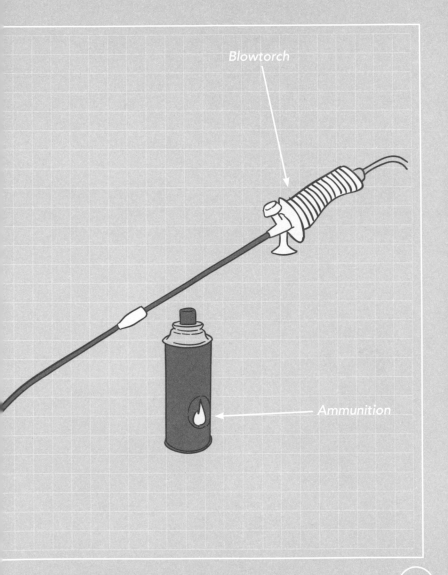

Blowtorch

Ammunition

SUFFOCATE THEM!

It may sound harsh, but we're at war with our unwanted greenery here, so it's inevitable that our weed treatments are going to hit weeds where it hurts. Here's a cheap and easy way to stop them in their tracks using sunflower oil.

Either dribble neat sunflower oil onto the weed, coating the leaves, or mix in a little powdered cinnamon, which has natural herbicide properties. The oil will smother the plant and is also biodegradable, so it will be broken down in your soil.

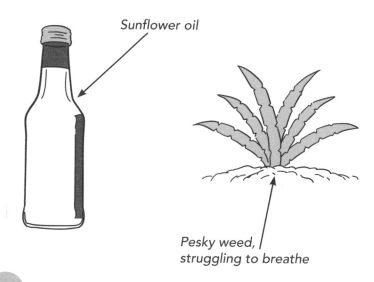

Sunflower oil

Pesky weed, struggling to breathe

PECK THEM!

Yes, you read that right! Grazing your weeds is a great way to get rid of them, and if you get some chickens you don't even have to do it yourself!

Chickens love to feed on anything green and will even take on backyard baddies like Japanese knotweed. To clear a large patch of this sort of weed, mow to a manageable height then let your feathered friends help themselves. The chickens will love the constant supply of fresh greens, you'll save on feed costs and you'll be getting eggs into the bargain.

Hungry chicken

Tasty knotweed

PROTECT YOUR NAILS!

Weeding means mucky fingernails – that's a given – but here's a hack to help you clean up more easily during your gardening sessions.

Gather together any leftover pieces of soap you have indoors – or go the whole hog and treat yourself to a fresh bar – and hang in a pair of tights from your outdoor tap. That way, when your hands start to get dirty, you can clean them as you work.

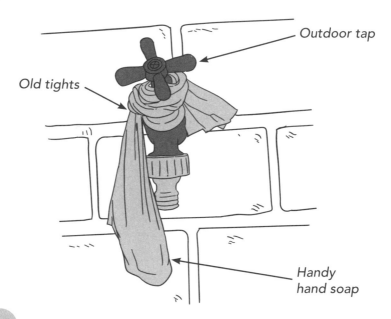

Outdoor tap

Old tights

Handy
hand soap

TOOL
HACKS

Tools are there to make our lives easier, but what if your rake's gone rusty or your hose is springing leaks? These cunning hacks will ensure that you keep your trusty tools in tip-top condition and even show you how to adapt your tools to make them extra useful. How did you manage without these hacks? Don't even think about it – those dark days are over now.

HANDY BRUSH-OFF HINT

To keep your tools as good as new, there's only one thing for it... you're going to have to clean them every time you use them. The good news is that you can make this easy by hanging a stiff brush next to your outdoor tap and making it a habit to brush off and rinse your tools every time you use them. Let them dry thoroughly before you put them away.

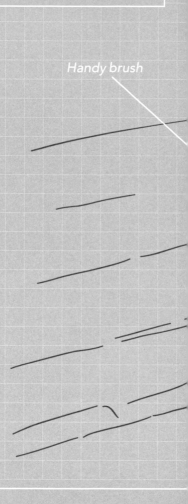

Handy brush

Outdoor tap

Sparkling spade

BUCKET HOSE STORE

If you leave your garden hose lying around on the lawn all year it'll develop kinks and leaks. Try this hack to keep your hose out of harm's way.

Turn a large bucket into a handy hose holder by fixing it to the wall of your shed with a couple of screws and washers. Wrap your hose around the bucket and pop your sprinkler inside it to keep it safe and tidy. Hose that for organised?!

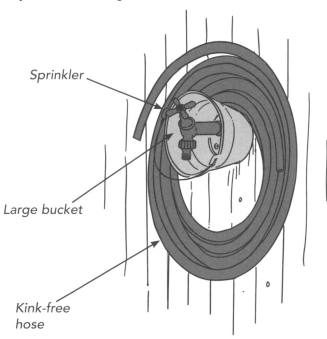

Sprinkler

Large bucket

Kink-free hose

GARDEN-FORK RULER

When plants need to be spaced a certain distance apart, don't waste time hunting for a ruler when you can turn your garden fork into one instead.

Just lay the fork down next to a tape measure and mark off measurements on the handle using permanent marker. Now you'll always have a ruler to hand when you're planting. Multipurpose magic!

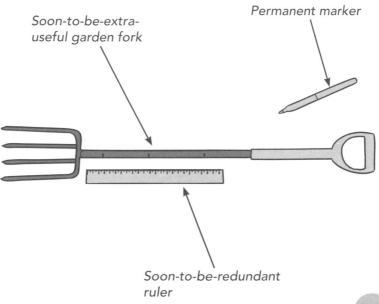

Permanent marker

Soon-to-be-extra-
useful garden fork

Soon-to-be-redundant
ruler

131

WHEELBARROW LOADING HACK

Whether you're transporting concrete, compost or an over-excited infant across the garden, your wheelbarrow is a lifesaver, but even your trusty one-wheeler can feel heavy when it's loaded to the brim. This tip for loading your barrow is so simple, but will make pushing your latest load a breeze.

Pile up most of your cargo over the front/wheel-end of the barrow and leave a void at the end nearest to you. The wheel – rather than your arms – will then take most of the load. (Note: not recommended for transporting infants!)

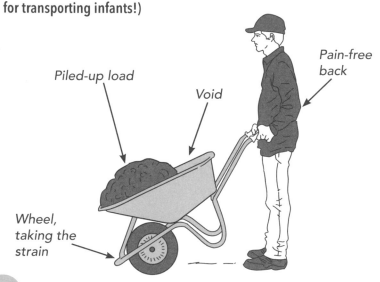

Piled-up load

Void

Pain-free back

Wheel, taking the strain

RAKE-HEAD TOOL RACK

Gardeners soon amass a collection of weird and wonderful hand tools – here's a great way of storing them all.

Simply remove and clean the head of an old steel rake and fix upside-down to the wall of your shed. (You can paint your rack if you like, but – you'll be glad to know – the rustic look works well.) Hang your hand tools on the prongs and you'll never lose your dandelion weeder again!

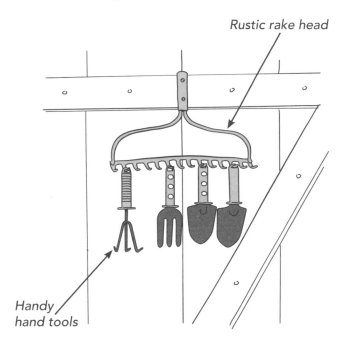

Rustic rake head

Handy hand tools

EASY VINEGAR RUST REMOVAL

The worst has happened and your favourite trowel is rusty, but don't despair: you can have it looking as good as new without reaching for the wire wool and elbow grease.

Start by soaking your trowel in vinegar for three hours, then scrub off the rust with a toothbrush. (It will come away easily.) Finish by soaking in a solution of two parts water to one part baking powder for five minutes, and rinse off. Dry your revitalised trowel thoroughly – using a hairdryer if necessary. Job done!

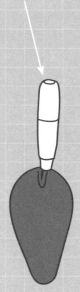

Rusty trowel (or spade, or fork)

Vinegar

Old
toothbrush

ICE-CREAM-SCOOP POTTING TOOL

This hack is great for when you're potting up small plants into equally tiny pots. It's a fiddly job and tricky to get the soil into the pots without scattering it everywhere. But here's how to do it.

If you use an ice-cream scoop instead of a trowel, you'll fill the pots much more neatly and avoid the soil clean-up operation afterwards. (Plus, next time you need to serve up ice cream, you've got a great excuse to use a trowel – it's win–win!)

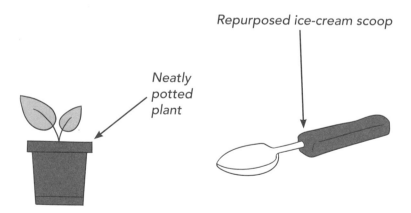

Repurposed ice-cream scoop

Neatly potted plant

SANDPAPER SHARPENING HACK

Sharp shears are speedy shears - try saying that three times quickly - then follow this tip to get great results every time you whip out your whetstone.

The blades of garden tools get covered in a layer of grime over time and it's really important to remove this before you sharpen them. Use a fine grade of sandpaper to buff up your blades before you sharpen and you'll be rewarded with super sharp shears every time.

Grimy shears

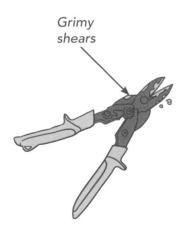

Gritty sandpaper

WHEELIE-BIN WATER BUTT

What could be greener than a water butt made out of a wheelie bin? (We're presuming that, being green-fingered, you have a bin of your own. If not, they're definitely worth the investment.)

All you need to do is buy a tap and rev up your drill. Lay your bin down and decide where to fit the tap – somewhere towards the base, of course! Drill a hole for it using a circular bit and fix the tap to the bin. Drill a larger hole in the lid to accommodate your downpipe and shift your butt into place, raising it up on bricks so that it's a handy height for your watering can. The lid will keep your water clean and pest free.

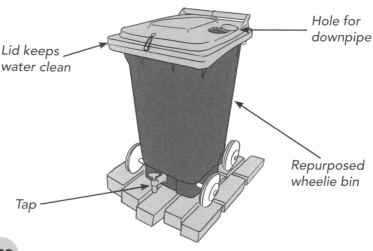

Hole for downpipe

Lid keeps water clean

Repurposed wheelie bin

Tap

PLANNING
AND
ORGANISING
HACKS

When it comes to planning and organising your planting, there are so many ways you can make your life easier. Here's a cunning combination of high- and low-tech hacks for everything from working out when to plant your veggies to making your own gardening oracle. And if you think there's never enough time to garden, turn to page 143 and think again…

PILL-BOX SEED STORE

If your precious seed collection consists of torn and tatty seed packets littering your shed floor, here's a much smarter storage option.

A pill box makes an ideal seed store and will keep your seeds safe and dry. Label each compartment, store the box on a shelf in your shed and you'll never lose your lobelias again. Just make sure you don't reach for the asters rather than the aspirin next time you have a hangover. (Bonus tip: moisten a toothpick and use it to lift smaller seeds out for planting.)

Toothpick
picker-upper

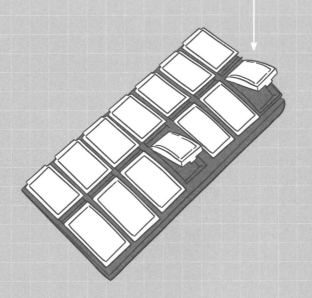

Perfect seed storage

SPEEDY SCHEDULING TIP

There was a time when the only way to plan your planting was to sit down with a calendar and your seed packets and spend the afternoon toiling over frost dates – so thank heavens for smartphones.

Save yourself time and trouble with a quick-and-easy app that can put together your planting schedule in a matter of minutes. Try the RHS's 'Grow Your Own' app for a tailor-made month-by-month to-do list with alerts reminding you to take action. You'll never miss your prime carrot-planting slot again!

Smartphone full of planting info

FLASH GARDENING BLITZ

Do you need more time to garden? Do you find yourself thinking that it's not worth pulling on your gardening gloves unless you've got an hour to spare? If so, try this technique for getting on top of things fast.

Set a timer for 15 minutes and get as much gardening done as you can before it goes off. (It's like speed dating, only with flowers and weeds.) It doesn't matter what you do, just so long as you do *something*. You'll be amazed at what you can get done in the time it takes to watch ten online cat videos.

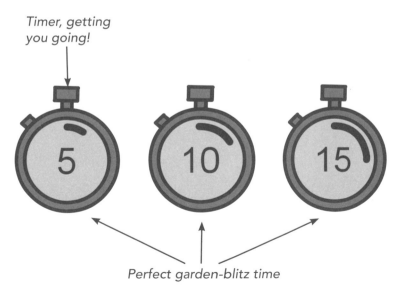

Timer, getting you going!

Perfect garden-blitz time

SUN-AND-SHADE SNAPS

This hack will show you how to work out where the sunny and shady spots are in your garden so that you can pick the right plants for each patch.

Take photos of your plot at intervals over the course of a day – early morning, mid-morning, lunchtime, etc. Do this for several days. If you take your photos from the same spot each time you can easily compare them to see which places will suit sun-basking blooms and which are best for their cool and shady cousins.

Sunny patch (not for shade-dwellers)

Photo of garden

Shady patch (not for sun-lovers)

RING-BINDER GARDENING ORACLE

There's a wealth of information out there on how to garden, but your plot is unique and the best way to learn what works for you is from experience. Become your own gardening guru and keep a journal of your gardening activities.

Use a ring binder to keep notes of plant sources, successes (yay!), failures (boo!), and sowing and blooming times, along with weekly observations and ideas of what you'd like to try next. You'll soon have plenty of wisdom to look back on.

Gardening oracle

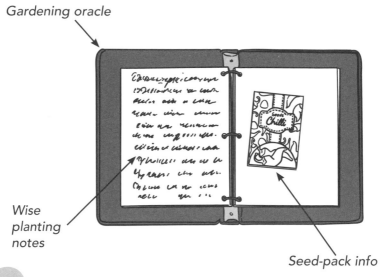

Wise planting notes

Seed-pack info

PLANT-TAG KEY-RING CLIP

What do you do with your plant labels? They don't exactly look great left in the pot with your newest purchase, but you don't want to lose all that precious info on how to avoid killing your plant either. Here's a great tip for keeping them organised.

Impale them on a large key-ring and hang them on a hook in your shed. It'll keep them tidy and handy for the next time you need to know how often to water your yucca.

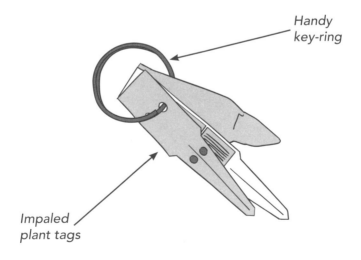

Handy
key-ring

Impaled
plant tags

HANDY HOSE HACK

If you're putting in a row of new plants - or planning a new flower bed – it can be difficult keeping everything in line if you're trying to judge it by eye.

An easy way to get a straight line every time is to lay out your hose and plant or dig alongside this. (You can also use your trusty hose if you want to put in a curved flower bed of course. Just lay the hose out in the perfect curve and dig out the shape you want.) Neat!

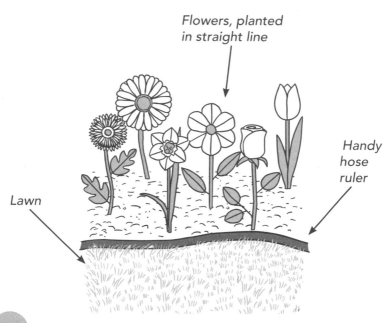

Flowers, planted in straight line

Handy hose ruler

Lawn

FINGER-TEST WATERING HACK

You could download an app to calculate watering times for you; you could invest in high-tech sensors that will alert you when the soil is dry; but the easiest trick of all is to use a low-tech sensor – your finger.

Just stick it – still attached to your hand, of course – into the soil next to your plant. Push it in up to your knuckle. If you can feel moisture in the soil around your finger there's no need to water. If you can't, you need to get the hose out (or perform a quick rain dance). Simple.

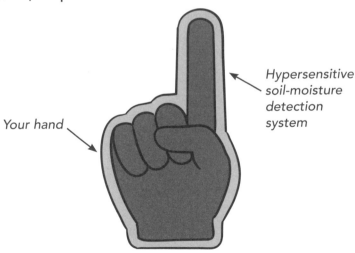

Hypersensitive soil-moisture detection system

Your hand

CLEVER COLOUR CONTRAST

You don't need to spend hours studying seed catalogues if you want to plan some punchy planting for your flower beds.

A simple way to max the impact of your floral displays is to pick two opposite colours from the colour wheel and use them together for contrast. Purples and yellows look great together, or try reds with greens, oranges with blues or hot pinks with lime greens. Your perfect planting will look like it's come straight out of the pages of a glossy magazine.

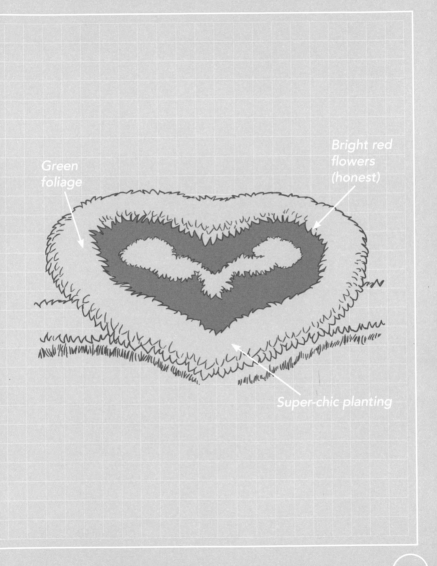

Green foliage

Bright red flowers (honest)

Super-chic planting

151

SHED AND GREENHOUSE HACKS

Your shed is your own private kingdom – and this chapter shows you how to organise that kingdom with a plastic-pipe tool rack and a funky funnel string dispenser. If you're lucky enough to own a greenhouse, we've included tips for you too. Whether you're keeping it warm in winter, cool in summer or fly-free all year round, there's a hack here with your name on it.

PLASTIC-PIPE TOOL RACK

It's all too easy to throw your long-handled tools, javelin-like, into the shed and hope they'll resurface next time you need them, but this great hack shows you how to make a storage rack using offcuts of plastic piping (think drain piping).

How many tools you want to house will determine the length of pipe needed. You'll need two 10-centimetre lengths for each tool. Once you've cut your pipe, fix two lengths of batten (2.5 x 5 cm or similar) horizontally to the shed wall, cut wide enough to accommodate all of your tools. Fix one at just above floor level and the other parallel, about a metre above the first. Attach your pipe pieces evenly across the batten, ensuring they line up vertically. Now you have a neat and tidy tool rack, enabling you to grab a broom and a rake at a moment's notice.

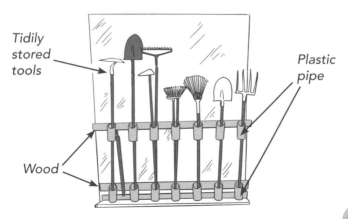

Tidily stored tools

Plastic pipe

Wood

WIRE-BASKET VEGGIE STORE

If you suddenly find yourself with potatoes (and onions and carrots) coming out of your ears your shed could be the perfect place to keep your surplus.

The best place to store your produce is up off the floor (of course), but don't use valuable shelf space: mount some wire baskets on your shed wall instead. Phew – looks like there's no need to cook 30 pounds of potatoes all in one go after all!

Shed wall

Plentiful potato harvest

Wire basket

FUNKY FUNNEL STRING DISPENSER

Here's a tip to stop your garden twine getting in a tangle – and it looks cool too. (You'll get lots of compliments next time you're, er, showing someone round your shed.)

Store garden string in funnels hung on your shed wall. Pop the ball of string into the top and trail the loose end down through the bottom. Hang a pair of scissors nearby and you can cut off the right length of string in seconds, rather than faffing around looking for the end of the ball. Complicated? Of course knot!

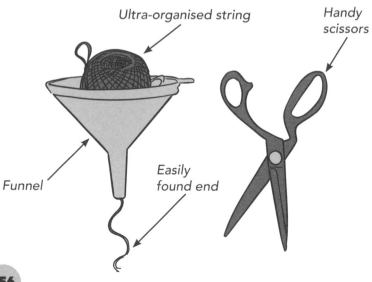

Ultra-organised string

Handy scissors

Funnel

Easily found end

GUTTERING POT STORE

I'm sure plant pots breed when we're not looking. It's all too easy for your collection to get out of hand – so how can you store them in winter, without them taking over the entire shed?

Just get hold of a short length of guttering and lay this along the back of your potting table. Then you can store pots in it, on their sides. They won't roll away and will be ready for you to grab when you start potting up your seedlings in the spring. Easy!

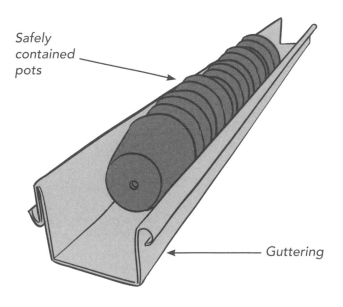

Safely contained pots

Guttering

EASY BUBBLE-WRAP INSULATION

Brrrrr! It's winter and things are getting chilly in the greenhouse, but here's a cheap way to keep the heat in: wrap your greenhouse in bubble wrap – on the inside, of course!

You'll need a giant roll of large-bubbled wrap for the best results. Measure the height of your walls first and cut panels to hang around those – secure with all-weather tape to the frame. Get a pal to help with the fun part – the roof – and your tender plants will have a much cosier home until the spring.

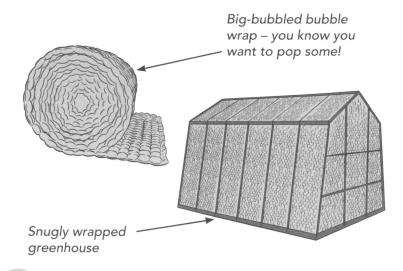

Big-bubbled bubble wrap – you know you want to pop some!

Snugly wrapped greenhouse

CLEVER COOLING HACK

Phew – it's the height of summer and you're worried your tomatoes are going to start roasting on the vine. This hack for cooling things down in the greenhouse might be low-tech, but it's cheap, effective and easy.

Grab your watering can and liberally water all the hard surfaces inside (paths, potting area, etc.). As the water evaporates it will take excess heat away with it. Cool!

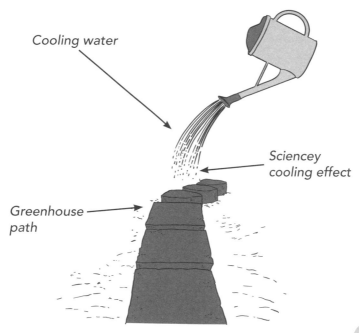

Cooling water

Sciencey cooling effect

Greenhouse path

PEBBLE-TRAY HUMIDIFIER

Unless your greenhouse is home to your prize cactus collection, you'll want it to be humid; but you don't need to buy an expensive humidifier – just try this simple hack instead.

Place trays of pebbles under your plantage, fill the trays with water so that it covers the pebbles and then allow our old friend evaporation (see page 159) to do the humidifying for you. You'll get a sultry atmosphere without plugging in any kit – saving pennies and the planet at the same time.

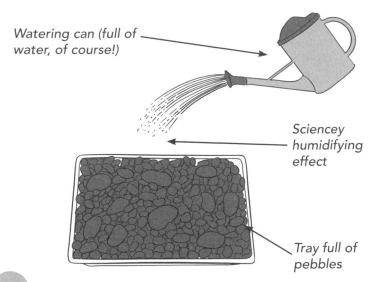

Watering can (full of water, of course!)

Sciencey humidifying effect

Tray full of pebbles

CARNIVOROUS PEST TRAP

If you want to keep pests out of your greenhouse, why not let your plants do the work for you?

Carnivorous trumpet pitcher plants will trap wayward flies and wasps, and look exotic all at the same time. Just keep the plants in a pot atop a saucer of rainwater and they will thrive, luring in flies and wasps with their scent. A mature plant can capture up to 3,000 wasps a season, so when the 'waspocalypse' comes it's a good one to have to hand.

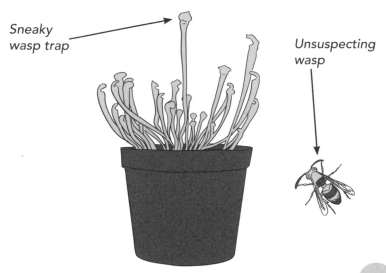

Sneaky wasp trap

Unsuspecting wasp

CUNNING COMPOSTER TOOL STORE

If you're lucky enough to have survived the waiting list and finally got an allotment, chances are you might not have inherited a patch with a shed for storing your tools.

Save yourself the trouble of carting your smaller tools to and fro every time you visit by keeping them in a spare, clean compost bin. If security isn't an issue, you can easily store a watering can, trowels and other hand tools inside your 'compost bin' – you can even use the little hatch for easy access. Clever you!

Compost bin, containing actual compost

Compost bin, aka undercover tool store

WILDLIFE-GARDEN HACKS

A garden bursting with wildlife doesn't just look good – it'll save you effort too. Buzzing bees and fluttering butterflies pollinate your flowers, busy earthworms till your soil, and – here's the clincher – hedgehogs, frogs and slow-worms all eat slugs. So, what are you waiting for? Go wild with these hacks and make your garden as creature-friendly as possible.

EASY APPLE BIRD FEEDERS

This is a nice project for kids – just make sure they're supervised, if necessary, when using the apple corer.

Remove the core from an apple, then make small holes all over the fruit. Push a sunflower seed into each hole. Hang up your feeder by tying some twine around the middle of a stick and passing it up through the apple's centre. Pop the core back in to hold the twine in place and voilà! One tasty, all-natural bird feeding station, complete with twig perch. The birds will be flocking to your garden in no time.

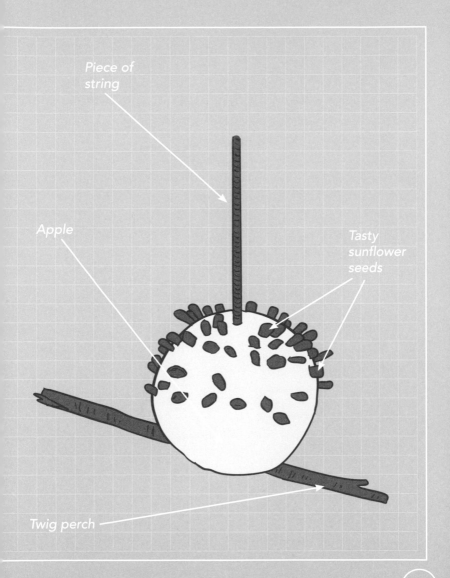

Piece of
string

Apple

Tasty
sunflower
seeds

Twig perch

165

ROPEY MOTH ATTRACTOR

Moths are great pollinators, so entice some over to visit with a bottle of red wine. There's no need to break out the Château Lafite – a bottle of supermarket plonk will do.

Add a kilo of sugar to the wine in a saucepan and heat, stirring until dissolved. Then soak metre-long strips of cloth in the mixture and hang them from branches in your garden. A late-night check will reveal some moth visitors (who may well be hung-over by morning).

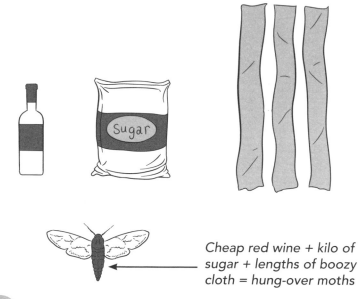

Cheap red wine + kilo of sugar + lengths of boozy cloth = hung-over moths

BIJOU BAMBOO BUG HOUSE

Ladybirds eat aphids – hurrah! – so encourage them to come and dine on the finest aphids in the street by making them a nest in your garden.

You could splash out on an elaborate ladybird house, but these useful creatures are as happy with a handmade rustic home as a lavish and pricey pied-à-terre. Cut some foot-long lengths of bamboo cane, lash them together with twine and wedge into the nook of a tree. The ladybirds will have a perfect place to rest when they're not feasting on your garden pests.

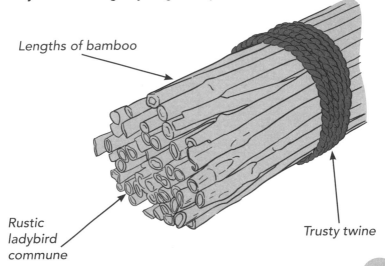

Lengths of bamboo

Rustic ladybird commune

Trusty twine

BUTLER-SINK POND

Ponds are great for attracting wildlife. Make a simple one from an old butler sink to avoid back-breaking digging and faffing with pond liners.

Position your pond where it will get good sunlight but some shade. Seal the plug in place with silicon glue and cover the bottom with gravel. Fill with rainwater and plant up with native pondweed in mesh containers to keep the water clear. Add some rocks piled up near the edge so that wildlife can get in and out, and you're done! Now just sit back and wait for the frogs to spawn.

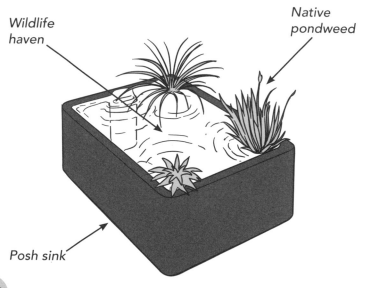

Wildlife haven

Native pondweed

Posh sink

HEDGEHOG HIGHWAY HOLE

Here's a great hack: hire a hedgehog to help in your war against slugs. Hedgehogs feast on the slimy plant-eating fiends, but they can only help if they can get into your garden in the first place.

Make sure your boundaries are hedgehog friendly by creating a hedgehog 'flap' – a hole no larger than a CD case is all they need. If you have walls, dig a small tunnel underneath. If you have fences, cut a hole for them to use instead. Your hedgehog highway is complete!

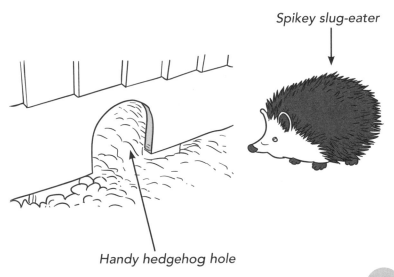

Spikey slug-eater

Handy hedgehog hole

ROCK-GARDEN WILDLIFE SHELTER

A rock pile will offer visiting wildlife shade, but plant it with some low-maintenance alpines and it'll look like a feature rather than a ruin.

Pick a site for your rock garden, remove any turf and cover with 15 cm of rubble. Next, put your larger keystones in place, securing with more rubble. Arrange smaller stones around these, leaving gaps for creatures to explore and inhabit. Add soil and leave to settle before planting up with alpines mulched with stone chippings. (*Sempervivum, aubrieta* and creeping thyme are all good choices.) A treat for the eye as well as the invertebrates!

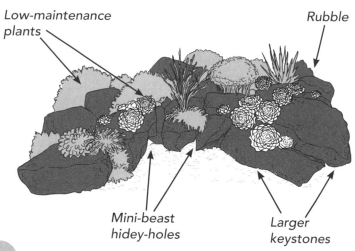

Low-maintenance plants

Rubble

Mini-beast hidey-holes

Larger keystones

BEE-FRIENDLY BLOOM TIP

Everyone knows that bees are beneficial garden visitors, but it's not so easy to remember which plants will attract them to your garden… right? Wrong! Read this hack and your garden will be buzzing with bees in no time.

Bees love:

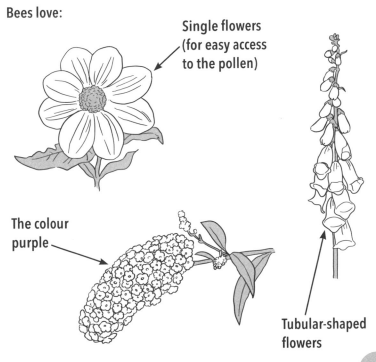

Single flowers (for easy access to the pollen)

The colour purple

Tubular-shaped flowers

WINTER WARMER ROOSTING POCKET

When the weather's so cold that your takeaway coffee comes with an ice pick, you can be sure that conditions are even harsher for your garden wildlife.

Offer small birds a cosy place to sleep by hanging up shop-bought roosting pockets or leaving out hanging baskets filled with moss and well-rotted compost in sheltered spots. (If you have a pet, grooming them outside will give birds a free supply of cosy roosting material too.) Coal tits, wrens and other small birds will find your overnight stopover a lifesaver, and a nearby supply of birdseed and nuts will go down a treat too. Bed *and* breakfast – perfect!

Cosy roosting pockets

Small, chilly birds

FUNGI-FRIENDLY RING-BARKING TRICK

A healthy insect population will bring other wildlife to your patch, and a great way to achieve this is to include some decaying wood in your garden. While taking an axe to your favourite apple tree might be a dramatic gesture, there's no need to go quite that wild. Try this hack on an unwanted shrub or tree instead.

Cut two thick rings around the trunk (about 20 cm apart) and strip away the bark between the cuts. This will kill the plant and allow it to decompose naturally, providing standing, decaying wood – a great home for insects, moss and fungi.

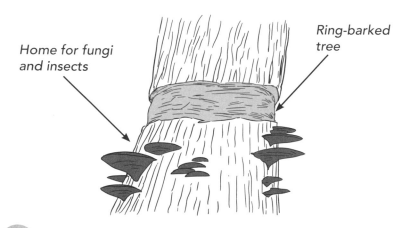

Home for fungi and insects

Ring-barked tree

EASY WORM-FEEDING STATION

They might not be the most attractive garden inhabitants, but worms are the hardest working creatures in your patch. Worms improve your soil to no end by aerating it and breaking down scraps. Encourage them to get to work on your soil by following this easy tip.

Just cut around the bottom of a plant pot (leaving a small 'hinge') to make a liftable lid and half bury the pot in your garden. Fill your pot with kitchen scraps, and worms will soon set up home nearby. Make more worm stations to attract more worms – easy!

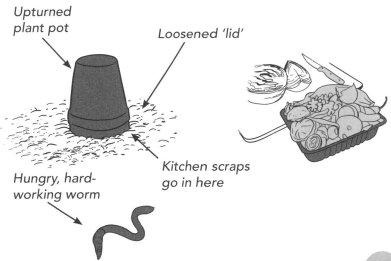

Upturned plant pot

Loosened 'lid'

Kitchen scraps go in here

Hungry, hard-working worm

LAWN HACKS

If you've heard the old adage 'You can either have a lawn or a life', don't despair… it's not true. You *can* open your curtains to a lush green vista every morning without spending hours maintaining your lawn (or moving in with a lawn slave). Read on for some handy hacks that'll leave your lawn glowing with health.

LEFT-CLIPPINGS NUTRIENT BOOST

Picking up your grass clippings is one of the most tedious lawn-maintenance jobs there is... so how about leaving them on the lawn instead?

If you cut your grass frequently, leaving short clippings on the lawn can return up to 25 per cent of the nutrients that grass growth has removed from the soil. The clippings will encourage earthworms, too, and they'll aerate your soil (see page 175). So don't rush for that rake; save time and let those clippings lie (or sprinkle them over the lawn, if your mower has kindly gathered them up for you!).

Nutrient-rich clippings left on lawn

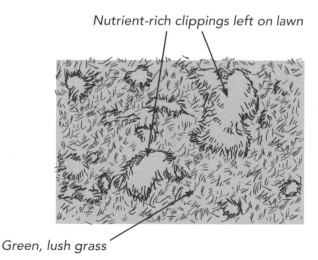

Green, lush grass

BREAD-KNIFE TURF TOOL

When you're laying turf in the garden there will always be some awkward edges that need to be trimmed, but the best tool for the job isn't in your shed – it's in your kitchen drawer.

Next time you need a tidy trim, use an old bread knife – it will saw neatly through the turf and is so quick and easy to manoeuvre that you'll have the job done in no time. You'll be on a roll!

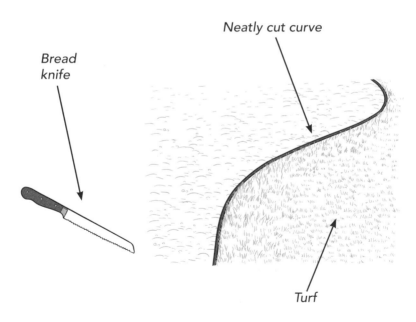

Neatly cut curve

Bread knife

Turf

RAKE SCARIFICATION TIP

Here's a task that involves a little work, but – like Christmas – it only needs to be endured once a year for great results.

Scarifying your lawn means removing any debris that's built up on the surface. You *could* buy a scarifier – but that's pricey and will clog up your shed, so get out there with your rake instead. Drag firmly across the grass, picking up any moss and debris that you collect as you go. Think of it as a workout – for you and your lawn – and you'll both see the benefits of a good scarification.

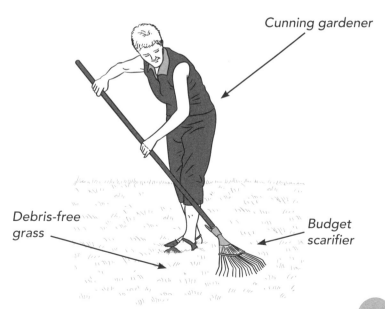

Cunning gardener

Debris-free grass

Budget scarifier

SPEEDY FORK AERATION

What you do on your lawn is up to you and your significant others, but chances are your grass sees a lot of action over the year. Whether it's running feet or rattan furniture, your lawn will end up compacted and need aeration every spring.

Don't invest in specialist equipment, just grab a garden fork and jab the prongs into your lawn. Jiggle about to open up the air holes and repeat every 6 inches. (If you're really conscientious, you can sprinkle a little loamy compost over the top and brush in for even better results.)

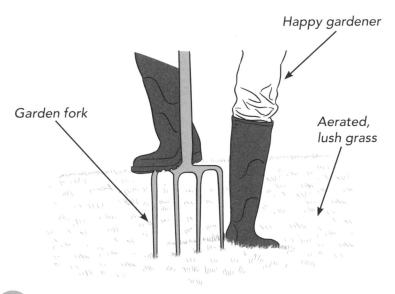

Happy gardener

Garden fork

Aerated,
lush grass

SUNKEN TRAMPOLINE TRICK

Here's a dilemma: you want to look out on a beautiful lawn every morning, but you also REALLY want your nippers to amuse themselves in the garden for hours on end. A trampoline would be perfect, but you don't want an enormous round lump of metal and rubber cluttering up your view.

Here's the solution: sink your trampoline so that it sits at lawn level. Yep, it'll take a little digging, but the pay-off is worth it – and you can always change your trampoline hole into a pond when your little darlings have outgrown it.

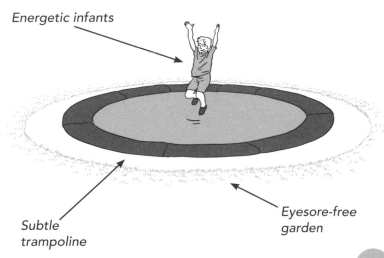

Energetic infants

Subtle trampoline

Eyesore-free garden

LAWN-WATERING WORM HACK

Healthy lawns host plenty of worms – they eat organic waste, aerate the soil and poop out nitrogen-rich castings – so make sure your lawn thrives by watering it thoroughly to encourage these useful inhabitants.

Water twice a week and worms will set up home in the damp, dark conditions beneath your grass. Watering plentifully has another benefit too – by letting water penetrate deeper into the lawn, you will encourage grass to send down deeper roots, making for stronger plants that can tap into natural sources of water farther down. Two reasons to get out that hose!

Lush, deep-rooted grass

Copious water

Perfect worm habitat

GRASS-CLIPPING MULCH

If you're wondering what to do with your grass clippings - and you've got too many to leave on the lawn (see page 177) - they'll make a great mulch for your sturdier veggies, such as potatoes and squash.

Grass cuttings are a great source of nitrogen, so a layer of these will boost your plants' productivity as well as suppressing weeds. (Just don't use more than 10 cm as too thick a layer will become a slimy slug magnet - yuck!)

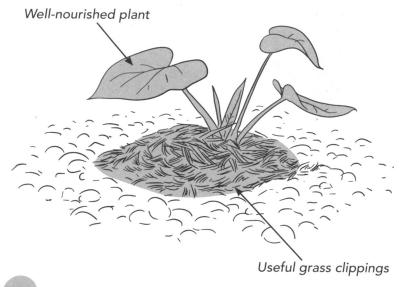

Well-nourished plant

Useful grass clippings

GROUND-COVER CHEAT

It's time we talked about the elephant in the room. There *is* a way you can get a great-looking lawn without ever having to mow again: cheat.

Artificial grass looks great and – these days – feels nothing like 1960s AstroTurf. It won't turn into a quagmire, get worn under the kids' swing set or turn into weird crop circles every time you leave garden equipment out overnight. It's not the best option for wildlife, but hang up a few bird feeders to assuage your conscience and lie back and relax while your neighbours are slaving away with their mowers.

Comfy chairs

Unblemished luxuriant grass

FINAL WORD

And that's it – well done, you! You are now a fully fledged Garden Hacker, ready to handle any challenge your plot throws at you in the blink of an eye, from decapitating your weeds to de-rusting your trowel. Be warned: with all these hacks under your belt, you may feel tempted to share your new-found wisdom with friends, family members and random passers-by. Don't be shy – go ahead! It's good to be a gardening guru. For what is a garden if not a reflection of the gardener – and now yours is productive, a little bit sexy and pest free.

If you have your own favourite gardening hacks to share with us, why not email them to auntie@summersdale.com? We'll look forward to reading them – from the comfort of our sunloungers, of course.

HACKS INDEX

FLOWER-TENDING HACKS

Compost Tea — 26
Cut-Flower Cocktail — 31
DIY Watering Can — 32
Fizzy Flower Treat — 35
Ice-Cube Orchid Fix — 25
Max Your Blooms — 24
Speedy Bucket Frost Protector — 34
Sticky-Tape Bug Blitzer — 29
Tea Mulch — 28
Vinegar Fertiliser — 30

GARDEN-DECORATION HACKS

Bright Block Bench — 96
Door-Key Wind Chime — 100
Magical Mirror Hack — 91
Painted-Stone Plant Markers — 95
Plant-Pot Lighthouse — 90
Punchy Patio Painting — 98
Quick Coastal Corner — 92
Tin-Can Lanterns — 94
Upcycled Chair Planter — 89

Wellie-Boot Hanging Garden — 99

LAWN HACKS

Bread-Knife Turf Tool — 178
Grass-Clipping Mulch — 184
Ground-Cover Cheat — 185
Lawn-Watering Worm Hack — 182
Left-Clippings Nutrient Boost — 177
Rake Scarification Tip — 179
Speedy Fork Aeration — 180
Sunken Trampoline Trick — 181

PEST-CONTROL HACKS

Aphid Spray-away — 56
Baking-Soda Ant Trap — 49
Black-Fly Bean Saver — 52
Bridal Berry Protection — 50
CD Bird-Scarer — 48
Citrus Slug Sorter — 53
Copper-Tape Plant Defender — 58
Crafty Companions — 60
Cutlery Patch Protector — 59
Move Those Mozzies — 55
Slippery-Pole Cat Deterrent — 54

PLANNING AND ORGANISING HACKS

Clever Colour Contrast — 150
Finger-Test Watering Hack — 149

Flash Gardening Blitz 143
Handy Hose Hack 148
Pill-Box Seed Store 140
Plant-Tag Key-ring Clip 147
Ring-Binder Gardening Oracle 146
Speedy Scheduling Tip 142
Sun-and-Shade Snaps 144

PLANT-HEALTH HACKS

Cinnamon Seedling Saver 37
Milky Mildew Fix 40
Pasta-Water Treat 41
Pine-Cone Drainage Hack 43
Poor-Soil Plant Bonanza 46
Shady Bolting Barrier 44
Tea-Tree Tonic 42
Winter-Cover Soil Booster 38

PLANTING HACKS

Berry-box Greenhouse 14
Cut-and-Dried Succulent Success 22
DIY Soil-Type Test 10
Easy Irrigation System 15
Eggshell Planters 9
Epsom-Salt Shock Absorber 19
Fridge-Top Germination Station 21
Honey Rooting Remedy 16
Nappy Water Retainer 18
Sandy Seed Solution 12

Stocking Plant-ties 20
Wine-Cork Seed Dibber 13

SHED AND GREENHOUSE HACKS

Carnivorous Pest Trap 161
Clever Cooling Hack 159
Cunning Composter Tool Store 162
Easy Bubble-Wrap Insulation 158
Funky Funnel String Dispenser 156
Guttering Pot Store 157
Pebble-Tray Humidifier 160
Plastic-Pipe Tool Rack 153
Wire-Basket Veggie Store 154

TOOL HACKS

Bucket Hose Store 130
Easy Vinegar Rust Removal 134
Garden-Fork Ruler 131
Handy Brush-off Hint 128
Ice-Cream-Scoop Potting Tool 136
Rake-Head Tool Rack 133
Sandpaper Sharpening Hack 137
Wheelbarrow Loading Hack 132
Wheelie-Bin Water Butt 138

TREE AND BUSH HACKS

Cane-Planting Guide 79
Cool Cutting Trick 82

DIY Dried Fruit   86
Easy Pruning (1, 2, 3)   84
Horizontal Hedge Trim   80
Leaf-Mould Soil Conditioner   87
Ornamental Grass Retainer   81
Quick Picking Tip   78
Speedy Cherry Snip   83
Tree Anchorage Hack   76

VEGGIE-PATCH HACKS

Bucket Potatoes   62
Cauliflower Cover-up   66
Epsom-Salt Tomato Sweetener   67
Handy Herb-Cubes Hack   68
Nettle Compost Quickener   65
Pepper Pinch-Out   73
Shoe-organiser Herb Garden   44
Speedy Radish Row-Marker   70
Stocking Onion Store   72
Strawberry Hanging Baskets   71
Tomato-Slice Seed Starter   64

WEEDING HACKS

Boil Them!   115
Burn Them!   122
Decapitate Them!   120
Dehydrate Them!   121
Dissolve Them!   118
Peck Them!   125

Protect Your Nails!   126
Rule Them Out!   116
Smother Them!   119
Suffocate Them!   124

WILD FLOWER HACKS

Coffee-Tin Seed Spreader   105
Free Seeds Hacks   102
Mason-Jar Soil Test   108
Paper-Towel Germination Cheat   111
Sandpaper Scarifier   110
Speedy Wild Flower Meadow   104
Wild (But Elegant) Planting Plan   107
Wild Flower Tyre Planter   112
Woodland Bulb Bonanza   113
Yellow-Rattle Grass Zapper   106

WILDLIFE-GARDEN HACKS

Bee-Friendly Bloom Tip   171
Bijou Bamboo Bug House   167
Butler-Sink Pond   168
Easy Apple Bird Feeders   164
Easy Worm-Feeding Station   175
Fungi-Friendly Ring-Barking Trick   174
Hedgehog Highway Hole   169
Rock-Garden Wildlife Shelter   170
Ropey Moth Attractor   166
Winter Warmer Roosting Pocket   172

IMAGE CREDITS